Language and Literacy Series
Dorothy S. Strickland and Celia Genishi, Series Editors

ADVISORY BOARD: Richard Allington, Donna Alvermann, Edward Chittendon, Bernice Cullinan, Colette Daiute, Anne Haas Dyson, Carole Edelsky, Janet Emig, Shirley Brice Heath, Connie Juel, Susan Lytle

(Continued)

LITERACY FOR LIFE

Adult Learners, New Practices

Hanna Arlene Fingeret
Cassandra Drennon

TEACHERS
COLLEGE
PRESS

Teachers College, Columbia University
New York and London

Published by Teachers College Press, 1234 Amsterdam Avenue, New York, NY 10027

Library of Congress Cataloging-in-Publication Data
Fingeret, Hanna Arlene.
    Literacy for life : adult learners, new practices / Hanna Arlene
Fingeret, Cassandra Drennon.
        p.   cm. — (Language and literacy series)
    Includes bibliographical references (p.) and index.
    ISBN 0-8077-3659-7 (hardcover : alk. paper). — ISBN 0-8077-3658-9
(pbk. : alk. paper)
        1. Literacy—New York (State)—New York—Case studies.
    2. Literacy programs—New York (State)—New York—Case studies.
    3. Literacy—United States—Case studies.   4. Literacy programs—
United States—Case studies.   I. Drennon, Cassandra.   II. Title.
    III. Series: Language and literacy series (New York, N.Y.)
    LC153.N7F56   1997
    379.2'4'09747—dc21   97-20388

ISBN 0-8077-3658-9 (paper)
ISBN 0-8077-3659-7 (cloth)

Printed on acid-free paper

Manufactured in the United States of America

04 03 02 01 00 99 98 97   8 7 6 5 4 3 2 1

This book is dedicated to our parents,
Blanche and Sidney Fingeret
and
Rod and Barbara Drennon
for their love and support

Contents

Acknowledgments

The students who participated in this project welcomed us into their lives and challenged us to move beyond the limitations of our own experience. We are indebted to their generosity; we hope we have appropriately respected their wisdom. We also appreciate all of the Literacy Volunteers of New York City (LVNYC) board members, staff, and volunteers who made the original study possible and have supported the development of this book. We thank everyone who helped us understand the implications of this work for adult literacy programs and practice, including Susan Joyner, Lennox McLendon, Susan Erno, Suzanne Cockley, and other members of the Virginia Association for Adult and Continuing Education; Liza Leiter and the teachers and students of North Metro Technical Institute in Acworth, Georgia; and Susan Hackney and the teachers and students of Coosa Valley Technical Institute in Rome, Georgia. Thanks to Susan Danin for support for us and for this project, and for her assistance and responses to drafts. We are indebted to the Literacy South staff—Page McCullough, Jereann King, and Pearl Shelby—and to Tom Valentine, Ron Cervero, Sharan Merriam, and numerous graduate students of the University of Georgia at Athens for continuous support and responses to drafts. We also want to thank Susan Lytle for initiating this publication, and our editors, especially Sarah Biondello and Carol Collins, for their perseverance and help.

Hanna Fingeret would like to thank many people for their continuous support through a very difficult time. Thanks to Blanche and Ted Pindus, Bruce and Rubi Fingeret, and Murray and Janet Fingeret. Thanks to Mike Katz, Eli Katz, Sheila and Victor Taube, Marsha and Doug Presnell-Jennette, Edward Hyman, Judith Abbott, Tema Okun, and Weigand Rodler. Many thanks to my healers: Dr. Marcey Shapiro, Joe Pfister, Lei Zheng, D. O., Janet Urman, Dr. Jim Telfer, Dr. Jay Dunbar, and Kathleen Cusick. Thanks to Rebecca Wellborn, Lysle Betts, Barbara Rhudy, and Deborah Green. Thanks to Jacqueline Cook and Mae Dick and to Richard J. Meyer. Thanks to Sondra Stein, always there for me. And deep thanks to Ed Lyons for everything.

Cassie Drennon thanks student colleagues at the University of Georgia —Mark Johnson, Donald Guthrie, Karl Umble, Judy Milton, Wanda Wilcox and Emuel Aldridge—who offered encouragement from beginning to end of this project. I am indebted to Dr. Barry Schwartz of the Department of Sociology. The ideas to which he exposed me came to shape this work profoundly. For reasons unique to each, I deeply thank family and friends: Rod and Barbara Drennon, Conrad Drennon, Steve Bricker and Janet Scagnelli, Don and Lindeve Hostvedt, Pat Tashjian, Karen Croft, Charlotte Hinson and Mike Boss, and, of course, David Bryant. Especially, I thank Ronna Spacone and Diane Foucar-Szocki for their love and for their support throughout the writing of this book. Their belief in me made all the difference.

LITERACY FOR LIFE

Adult Learners, New Practices

Introduction

This is a snapshot in time of the lives of five adults—Lawrence, Marsha, Don, Ann, and Maria—including the story of their participation in a literacy program and their tales of change, courage, shame, struggle, and triumph. Their names have been changed to protect their privacy. The group is diverse, reflecting the fact that adults who come to literacy programs are diverse; their lives are complex and interesting. They negotiate the world in many different ways, including, for some, being productive workers, caring parents, and active community members.

As adults develop new ways of using literacy in their lives, they change their lives. Creating change often is difficult, even for adults who have a multitude of resources. Adults who want to develop their literacy abilities often have fewer resources, yet they frequently face the challenge of change with determination and courage.

Lawrence, Marsha, Don, Ann, and Maria differ from each other in many ways; they are diverse ethnically, linguistically, socially, and psychologically. However, in 1990, these five adults shared some goals around literacy development, and they joined hundreds of others to attend Literacy Volunteers of New York City (LVNYC).

This book started as a study of the impact of participation on the literacy abilities and practices of students in LVNYC in 1990 (see Appendix for explanation of the methodology of the larger study). Impact studies usually document *what* changes students ascribe to their participation. As we talked with students about their participation in LVNYC and its impact on their lives, we were confronted with an impressive array of narratives of change processes and limits. As our work progressed we became increasingly interested in *how* change happens, and why some people change in certain ways rather than in other ways.

It became clear that *impact is situational.* Assessment of learner progress in many literacy programs focuses on students' technical skills (e.g., decoding, word recognition), as if those technical skills were applied the same way in all circumstances. However, we found that technical skills are applied differently, depending upon the situation and the person. We also found that literacy is not only *in* situations, but literacy change has an

1

impact *on* the situation, as well. When an adult who has not used literacy in a situation does so for the first time, the situation—and the social relationships within the situation—change. Therefore, it became necessary to understand students' lives in depth in order to appreciate the dimensions of change and the relationship between change and program participation. Since this has been an evolving understanding on our part, the research reported here only begins to explore learners' rich cultural, linguistic, and social backgrounds.

We have organized this book into three major sections. In Section I we present profiles of five program participants and the instructional program at LVNYC. In Section II we introduce a framework for understanding the processes in which these adults appear to participate as they move towards increasingly broad-based change. In Section III we explore the implications of this framework for literacy students, educators, and others interested in personal change in our complex social world. We hope that readers will move back and forth among the sections, connecting the more theoretical material in Section II with the lives of the adults profiled in the first section and with the implications for their own practice as it may be reflected in Section III.

SECTION I

Profiles

Each student in our profiles tells a unique story, and helps us understand different facets of change. Their backgrounds and prior schooling experiences give us insight into the factors that contributed to their problems with literacy practices as adults, and help us understand their attitudes toward schooling and learning today. Here we see the beginning of tensions relating to literacy, as well as developing resources for lifelong learning. Students' experience with LVNYC, or life inside the program, helps us see the relationship between the resources students bring and those the program provides. We can see the role of effective instruction in facilitating change, and the importance of relationships that are forged in this domain. Students' experience outside the program provides insight into the role of environment and context in the change process. We also see how learners choose to engage in some new literacy practices, but not in others. Further discussion of social relationships helps us understand the centrality of community in the change process. The LVNYC instructional program is the subject of the final profile in this section, helping us understand more details of students' experiences in the program.

1

Lawrence: "I Want to Become Something"

Lawrence is 30 and lives with his parents above the Italian deli they own in the Bronx. Every chance he gets, Lawrence helps his father in the deli by putting beer and soda away or by mopping the floors after closing.

Lawrence describes his regular job at the local Transit Authority as "pushing a broom, picking up orders, and driving a fork-truck." Lawrence hopes that if he improves his reading he will be able to rise within the ranks of the Transit Authority to a conductor's position. "I want to move up," he explains. "I don't always want to be down on the ground."

Lawrence wants to move "up" but not away. Strong family relationships and cultural traditions keep him from considering a move away from his parents' home even though some of his friends think that more independence would be good for him. Lawrence explains, "I can't leave my mother and father. What they went through with me, God! . . . I would never leave them . . . why leave them? What they did for you, you should do for them." Consequently, Lawrence's days are long as he manages work and home responsibilities along with attending the literacy program two evenings each week.

Prior Schooling Experiences: "Nobody Read My Stories"

Lawrence traces his reading difficulties back to early school years when his behavior, family circumstances, and conditions within the educational system all seemed to work against his progress. He recalls that he often behaved "wildly" in school. Although he spent a lot of time distracted from his lessons, he was viewed as somewhat of a leader among his classmates because he was willing to speak out:

> I was a wild kid when I was a little kid. . . . I didn't bother to pay
> attention to teachers. . . . School was boring. It was 30 or 40 kids in

class. I didn't pay attention—my mind was somewhere else . . . I
was too wild. When it came down to it, I was the one that would
speak up. What's right and wrong? And they didn't like it. I caused
a lot of trouble because some people followed my feelings, you
know.

As Lawrence sees it, there were teachers who "just put their time in
and didn't care." He remembers an instance when he confronted his teachers with the opinion that their classes were boring and nobody was learning anything. "Everybody's just goofing off," he told them. When he was
14, Lawrence's tendency to speak out was viewed as enough of a discipline problem that he was restricted to attending classes only half-days.
In the afternoons he went to a program offered through a local university
designed especially for teenagers experiencing reading problems. Lawrence
quickly became bored with the program, however, because he was asked
to read from books obviously designed for students at lower grades. His
attempts to keep up with the other students on his grade level were hindered by the fact that, unlike many of his classmates, Lawrence did not
receive additional reading help at home. His immigrant parents read and
spoke only Italian. Eventually Lawrence enrolled in a vocational high
school program and ended up receiving a graduation certificate. When
explaining this, he mused, "I don't know how the hell I got that!" In other
words, Lawrence understood that he had been passed through the entire
system without really being able to perform the work.
    Lawrence recalls that reading troubles as a child did not stand in the
way of his love for writing short stories. Although he mostly kept his writing
private, one teacher stands out in his memory for the way she became his
ally, sharing the pleasure he experienced through creating stories.

When I was a kid I started writing but nobody read my stories. The
only one I showed was my teacher. She liked it because I always
wrote about love stories. . . . She bought me a big scrapbook, this
big. But I would write . . . you know, like writing love stories and
she would correct my spelling. . . . She was so happy. She said keep
writing more.

Although Lawrence enjoyed writing when he was young, he gave it up
when he started working and did not write for enjoyment again until he
entered the program at Literacy Volunteers of New York City (LVNYC).
    During the years between high school and entering the literacy pro-
gram as an adult, Lawrence put attention to his reading problem behind

him, and focused instead on earning a living. He worked a series of jobs in restaurants, catering halls, and bars, before getting his present job with the Transit Authority.

According to Lawrence, it was not one particular event that triggered his wanting to join an adult literacy program. He describes instead how he came to a realization about his future: "One day if I ever get married and my kid comes up to me and asks me to read, you know, I don't want . . . [him or her] to think that reading's not important, you know." Lawrence's vision of the future includes children, a house in the country, and a business. Lawrence believes that he must strengthen his reading and writing abilities if his vision is to become real:

> You need it when you go and sit down and you got lawyers and you know, you're opening the business. You want to know what those words are. You don't want to always say, "Excuse me, can you break it down for me?" You don't want to look like a jerk, you know.

Lawrence first learned about Literacy Volunteers of America from an advice column in the *Daily News*. He asked his best friend, Mario, a close confidant since childhood, to set up his first appointment and to accompany him there. Lawrence says he was nervous the first time he went to LVNYC. He was afraid that the program would be like school—too many people in a room trying to get help from too few teachers. Based on his past experience, he also worried that the content would be irrelevant to his interests:

> I was in a program around where I lived. . . . It wasn't working out. . . . I felt very uncomfortable, because "Who lives around the block? I live around the block?" Give me a break. I mean, I'm not here [for] "who lives around the block." I'm here to read. I mean, it was like one of those movies. There are courses that do help and there are courses that don't. You got to be very careful today.

He felt reassured when he was assigned to a small group of both young and old people, and thought, "They came down to better themselves, so you could do the same." He found a group in which he was like others rather than different from them, and the potential for real change seemed to exist. Lawrence reflects: "Everybody's afraid to make that first step. And then I do [and] sometimes I am afraid. I choke off sometimes because you get scared sometimes. But then."

Life Inside the Program: "I Just Want to Go with the Flow"

Lawrence had been in the program for 7 months when he sat down to be interviewed for this study. When he first came to LVNYC, he was told that he was reading at a fourth-grade level. When the interviewer asked Lawrence if he felt he was making progress since he started the program, he replied ambivalently, "Yes, in a way, but then in another way sometimes it feels like it's boring." He says that "effort" matters if he is going to better himself, but adds, "I just want to go with the flow, do what I got to do and get out. That's it. That's me. I don't want to start no trouble. When I start trouble, forget it."

Although Lawrence talks about the program with ambivalence, he experiences a level of support, assistance, and respect for his writing that he would not receive otherwise. His referring threateningly to his capacity to "start trouble" within the program is reminiscent of the resistant behavior that distinguished him in school. As a child, Lawrence was "pushed through" an educational system that he perceived as unresponsive to his needs. As an adult, Lawrence approaches his learning with new authority and a greater measure of control. Readiness to learn and possibilities for the future now contribute momentum for him to push himself through the literacy program he attends voluntarily. Lawrence wants to feel he has choices and that he can realize his potential for change:

> I want to become something because I want to be able to move on. Just want to become something. I don't know what but I want to become. . . . I don't want that much. . . . I just want to own my own house somewhere in the country. I like kids. . . . I like to travel, see the world. I'd like to own my own business. One day it might happen. That's something, you know.

Lawrence's demeanor shifts throughout his interviews according to the subject of conversation. Often sarcastic, he doesn't hesitate to tell the interviewer that her questions seem stupid. Generally he projects the persona of a tough guy who has seen and done it all.

However, when the conversation turns to his tutoring group, a gentle quality overtakes Lawrence. His remarks turn serious, thoughtful, and self-revealing. Lawrence describes a playfulness among members of his tutoring group and understands this to represent a form of caring. He explains that the way everyone picks on each other in a "nice" way serves an important purpose because "it gives that person the courage to see that we care for that person and they feel more positive in themselves, you know."

According to Lawrence, group members help each other. "It's like a family, you know. It's great." Norms have developed within Lawrence's group. Certain patterns of relating are respected among the members. As they work toward a shared goal, they see at least glimpses of themselves in one another and this affinity serves to bind them. Lawrence explains, "I know where they been at. They been hiding in a closet just like me. Afraid to speak out and call for help." With this realization, Lawrence is careful to function like others in the group and not call attention to himself in ways that would set him apart from others. He explains,

> In any group, you don't show off. It's not right to show off. Help each other out but don't show off because it hurts them more. I mean it gives them more [incentive] to work harder because you're doing better but don't show off. It's not right to show off because then you're feeling like they're stupid. But they're not stupid. They're smarter than you. You'd be amazed.

From time to time LVNYC sponsors reading celebrations. Adult students come together and read stories they have written in the program. The celebrations take place in public settings such as churches but retain a sense of privacy because only fellow students, program staff, friends, and family are invited to attend. Program staff decide who will be invited to read at the celebrations. The celebrations often feel like public situations in that there is a sense that one's abilities are open to the scrutiny of outsiders. Although Lawrence will not be reading at the upcoming celebration, he explains how he would feel if he were: "I heard it's a big crowd and I may choke up. . . . I choke up sometimes. . . . Like, I'm in a group I could talk and when it gets too big, I get nervous."

Lawrence speaks from experience. One time he read his work in front of a group of 40. Although he was nervous, the experience was overwhelmingly positive for him.

> It made me feel very happy. And I felt like crying because they were listening to how I felt. Like my, my heart . . . a little door was opening. And the people were listening and they wrote little notes. I have it in my scrapbook. Everything's in my scrapbook. You know . . . they wrote a lot of things. And the [other] people that was reading, I wrote to them. . . . And I wrote everybody "Good luck, I think you're great! Keep up the good work! If you believe in yourself you could believe anything you could do." Things like that.

At the time of these interviews Lawrence has just finished writing a 40-page story about a basketball player. Tutors have helped him edit the story and correct spelling errors. He has finished recopying it to include the changes. Writing instruction at LVNYC emphasizes meaning over mechanics and when Lawrence describes his own writing process, his words reflect this emphasis:

> I know when I keep writing I can't stop, because it's all in your mind. . . . It's all in your head and you keep writing, keep writing. . . . I did go back after I finished and then I put the periods, the dots, and the quotes and the commas. . . . I love writing stories. I don't know why. I wrote a lot. I wrote some short ones. I got me a scrapbook. I bought me a scrapbook and I put all my stories in there and everything.

Writing is significant for Lawrence, not simply because it allows him to create stories or fill out job applications, but because of what it says about him in a much larger sense. It becomes apparent, listening to Lawrence, that writing provides the *evidence* that he is a competent, capable person. He says, "At least I got something to show my kids . . . all my sister's kids that I did something. At least I proved to myself that I could write."

Life Outside the Program: "The Future's Right Here"

Lawrence wakes up early in the morning to travel an hour and a half by train to his job. He says he reads the newspaper on the train—usually the *Daily News* or the *New York Post* because he finds these easier to read than the *New York Times*. Lawrence especially likes to read the sports pages to keep up with the game scores and other related news. Then at the end of the day, he picks up a small paper from one of the nearby counties, so that he can catch up on local news. As Lawrence puts it, he likes to read about the "funny little things that happen in a small town."

Lawrence punches his time card when he gets to work and then he says he likes to spend a few minutes "bullshitting" with the guys over breakfast at a nearby diner. Reading the menu at the diner does not pose a problem for Lawrence, who has become accustomed to the selections. "Egg Sandwich, BLT, it's easy," he says from experience. Back on the job, reading tasks are less predictable and pose more of a challenge. For instance, in order to know what he has to do on any given day, Lawrence reads a set of work orders containing both code numbers and words. He says that when he first started his job, reading the work orders was difficult. But he says, "I learned from people doing it. I learned from other people that were showing me." Lawrence also has to be familiar with all the safety rules of his company. He shows his interviewer a set of booklets with small type covering all the safety rules and explains that each day the management asks employees to focus on a different rule: "They give you the number like this . . . like 120: 'To Apply Pump Handle and Hand Brakes.' So the safety rule today is 120. So they would say, you look it up in the book and you read . . . and you read it to yourself."

Lawrence believes that the company is seeking to protect itself by having employees focus on a different safety rule each day. In other words, if the employees understand the rules they may be more likely to avoid accidents and the company may reduce its risk of lawsuits. Some of the safety rules are more difficult to read than others. Lawrence explains that when he has trouble with one, he will "cross and ask the next guy 'what does that word mean'?" Sometimes the company will provide a special training class on particular safety rules. Lawrence explains, "You sit for an hour in class, they'll show you a video and explain to you everything that's in this book in the video."

For Lawrence, the most important safety rules concern handling hazardous materials with care. "That's my life there," he says. He knows that if he becomes a conductor one day, he will have to learn even more safety rules and a lot more math since he would be dealing with money. He says he would also have to learn how to spell the names of stops so that he could read and announce them on the public address system. "Glenwood . . . or Umstead . . . or Croton on the Hudson or . . . so many stops that you know you got to announce. You got to read that."

Lawrence has many stories about life-style changes that coincide with his participation in LVNYC. New literacy abilities, growing feelings of self-confidence, and an emerging personal vision of the future are all linked in such a way that change occurs to some extent in most aspects of Lawrence's life. Lawrence provides a glimpse of the "before and after" in this portion of an interview:

> What would I have done before if I didn't come to the Program?
> . . . I would have gone out and watched, or go upstate, go down to Manhattan, go to South Street Seaport—I would have gone out. I wouldn't have stayed home. . . . [Now] I stay home to write. . . . I'm doing more better now than I was before. I'm communicating with a lot of people now than before. When somebody talks to me, I listen, I don't turn around.

As Lawrence engages in new literacy practices, he finds the world becoming a lot less mysterious. The first time he used an automatic teller machine (ATM), for instance, Lawrence remembers being scared. Nevertheless, he was able to read everything on the screen and follow the directions in order to receive $20 in cash. He remembers thinking to himself, "Wow, that was fast. . . . Where's the money coming from, you know? Because that's so easy. At the end of the month you see, Oh, that $20 [is] missing out of that checking account." In another instance, Lawrence took the initiative to apply for a library card. After filling out the application form, he asked the librarian, "How long do I have to wait?" When she told him he could get books right away, he remembers thinking to himself, "Oh, God, I don't believe it! The future's right here."

The reason Lawrence wanted a library card in the first place was so that he could check out a book that would help him learn to type his short stories. In addition to learning to type, Lawrence says he is taking piano lessons to calm his nerves. He now compares learning to play the piano with learning to read: "Where's the A? Where's the C? It's fun. You learn how to read notes. It's the same thing [as] reading the book because it's got, you know, the words on the bottom and you read it. And I like music . . . it calms me down."

One significant life-style change for Lawrence occurred when he joined a gym and a weight loss support program. Over six months, he lost 48 pounds and learned for the first time to shop alone for new clothes. According to his friend, Mario,

> He never used to really go out and buy clothes. He would say to my wife and me, "Come on down here. Let's go. I want to buy a suit. Does this look good on me? What should I buy?" So, it's kind of like a big accomplishment going there buying clothes, buying shoes.

According to Lawrence, however, his biggest accomplishment so far is going on a vacation by himself to Cancun: "First time I went in and booked something and you know, did it on my own. . . . I was smiling."

Relationships and Social Support: "Boy, You've Got a Lot of Guts"

Lawrence and Mario have been friends since elementary school. When assigned to different high schools, the two continued to "hang out" together, yet Mario says that he never realized Lawrence had a reading problem. "It never crossed me and it never seemed that way," he says. Mario explains how he came to realize Lawrence's circumstances:

[He was] going through a school just like I was, at different schools. He said he was passing in everything else, so you never think that there's a problem because usually they . . . will not promote you. And, but one thing happened when I was 17, I went into the service. So, for eight years . . . I didn't see him that much. I wrote him once or twice. Not that much because I'm not that much of a writer. And then when I came back, we started back in our relationship again and we all used to do a lot of things. And then there were times that [Lawrence would say], "Mario, could you help me with this application? Just fill this out." [And I would say,] "Sure, no problem."

Lawrence passes a lot of time with Mario and his wife, Paris. He visits their house regularly and the three talk, watch TV, and eat meals together. On Saturday nights they go to a night club or to the movies. Mario thinks that loneliness is an issue for Lawrence: "If he had that extra type female lady encouragement, he could do, I think, even higher bounds because he'll have somebody." A year earlier, Lawrence had broken up with a girl-friend. In Mario's opinion, the breakup was the best thing that could have happened for Lawrence at the time: "She wouldn't even help him with reading or nothing. She wasn't interested. That's something he didn't need. He needed somebody more supportive."

In the absence of a more supportive girlfriend, Mario and Paris continue to be available to Lawrence for social life, emotional support, and practical assistance. As Lawrence's reading and writing practices develop, Mario develops new respect for his friend's abilities:

He learns new things and he's happy when he comes home. He says, "Hey I wrote this story. What do you think?" I say, "It sucks." (Laughter) "No, I say, 'It's good.'" . . . One time he wrote something and I says, "Lawrence, you wrote this? You could help me. You don't need to go down there no more. You could help me," I told him. . . . He says, "But wait, . . . let me show you what I did." So he showed me his work and [how] he corrected it. . . . And I said, "Lawrence, if you do this, you could teach me."

Most of Lawrence's friends and family members appear supportive of his participation in the literacy program. He explains, "When I talk to my friends . . . they say 'Boy, you've got a lot of guts to do what you're doing now.'" When asked how his family is responding to his being in the program, Lawrence says, "They're 100% with me."

In spite of the support people show for his attending the program, Lawrence's relationships sometimes suffer as a result of changes he is undergoing:

> I show [my writing] to my friends and family. But you know it's like . . . it's great to show them but then they get aggravated because they feel like boy, this guy's achieving. You know, he's getting places. Article in this paper, article in that. And I don't like to do that because I can see . . . I can feel a person's vibes.

Mario believes that, as a result of Lawrence's new reading and writing practices, their relationship "became a lot stronger in a way." He continues, "And then in another way, I wanted to break the chain—I wanted him to do things more on his own." Mario describes how Lawrence used to have a block about getting close to people, but

> now he doesn't have to put up that block no more because now he's seen that he could do it. He did it with his weight, his reading, his application process. But the relationship with me and him is still the same as it was. It's just that now he's doing more things on his own.

Lawrence's change in confidence and attitude has also manifested itself at work. He is not engaging in many new literacy practices per se, but changes in his way of relating to co-workers and supervisors reflect the deeper process of change in which he is engaged:

> I stick up for my fellow workers and me [now], like talking to my foreman or my superiors. . . . Before, I keep my mouth shut because I want to go farther at my job. . . . [Now I feel that] if you don't speak up, they're going to walk all over you. So I speak up for me and the people I care [about].

After having felt silenced for years, Lawrence now believes in his own voice.

2

Marsha: "Something in Me
Keep On Pushing"

Marsha, an African American woman in her mid-20s, shares an apartment in a large Manhattan housing project with her older brother and sister. Marsha has lived in this neighborhood since high school, and she says it's the kind of neighborhood where "babies are having babies" and drugs are easy to come by. When Marsha walks through the neighborhood she avoids making eye contact with her neighbors and rarely talks with them. Children play against the backdrop of graffiti and men shoot dice in the corner, and few take notice of her anyway.

Marsha likes to think of herself as different from most who live in her apartment complex. Not only is she different now, but she carries vivid images of what she intends to become. These images include working in an office somewhere and "dressing like a working woman": "I feel I want something in my life besides having a baby or [living] on welfare. . . . I want my freedom." Marsha imagines the day when people will say, "Look at Marsha, you know, she's doing good for herself, she got a good job, she got her own apartment, she looking good, you know, things like that." She has taken steps to make her dreams a reality, including taking literacy classes at LVNYC.

In contrast to the street life below, Marsha's sparsely furnished eighth-floor apartment is clean, quiet, and orderly. The few well-worn furnishings contrast with a new TV in the center of the living room. On the mantle, a collection of family pictures is flanked by two red plastic poinsettia plants that were once Christmas decorations at the bakery in which she works. There are no books or magazines around the apartment, except for a neat stack on the kitchen table—two LVNYC publications that include stories she has written along with the notebooks she takes to and from the program. Normally she keeps her notebooks under her mattress; she took them out to share with the interviewer. Marsha spoke softly with her interviewer because her brother, a sanitation worker for the city who had just gotten off his shift, was sleeping in the next room. Her sister, who was expecting a baby, was sleeping in another bedroom. She explained the relationships within the household:

> It's like we're doing our own thing. You know, we give each other respect. We have our own privacy, you know, and everything. And then when it comes down to the house thing, we all together taking care of the house to make sure everything is correct.

The life-style Marsha dreams about includes her own apartment decorated according to her tastes. She says she would "dress nice, you know. Go out, eat lunch out with the girls—things like that, you know, instead of just going, wearing the same thing everyday to work." She continues:

> I like to see myself more independent, that where I have my own apartment, I have a good job, I'm coming and going, paying my bills, have no problems, and living a life that I wanted to live. That's what I would like. And peaceful. And, you know, going to church, and this and that.

According to Marsha, a good job with benefits stands between her and the life-style she would like to be enjoying. At the time she was interviewed for this study, she had been working for hourly wages at the same bakery for three years. Experience has taught her that problems with literacy make it difficult for her to compete for other jobs, particularly those that offer benefits. She explains,

> It's so hard, I think, for people who can't read or write because you got to have so much the skills sometimes and then you know these jobs out here. . . . They're always saying, "Well, we'll keep your application for six months," or whatever. . . . I've been looking around, putting in applications and hoping that something comes through.

Marsha would like to improve her reading and writing so that she will be more qualified for higher-paying and more secure jobs that offer benefits. She says, "I'm getting older and not younger and if I want to get . . . a better job, I've got to educate myself first to be able to get this type of job, whatever, that I'm looking for." Marsha also wants to continue her journal writing:

> The only thing that's holding me back is my reading because I like writing. And if only I can learn how to spell and read these words as I write. Like some people keep diaries, they write about every-

thing that happened and their days. I would love to do something
like that, who knows. I could have wrote a book about myself by
now.

Also, Marsha says that she would like to be able to read books cover to
cover, especially books that are exciting or those that everyone seems to
be talking about.

> But it's one book that's out that's very popular that I see a lot of
> people, I mean a lot of Black people, reading it now. This Black
> woman she wrote this book about how the Black woman should be
> and this and that. . . . I think a real heavy book and I want to get
> that book. . . . Something in me keep on pushing me to get that
> book and to really, you know, read it.

Prior Learning Experiences: "No Proper Education"

Marsha says that growing up was "hard." Sometimes she stayed with her
grandmother while other times she lived with an older cousin. Intermit-
tently she would return home to live with her mother. Marsha never knew
for sure why she was sent to live with relatives but she guesses it had something to do with the notion her mother had of her as "wild." Because she
moved around so much, Marsha attended several different elementary
schools and her memories from this era are sketchy. The only diploma
Marsha says she ever received is from a Catholic school where she completed the eighth grade.

When she reached the tenth grade, her mother sent Marsha to the
Job Corps program in upstate New York for two years. She and her mother
had seen television commercials indicating that the Job Corps could teach
her useful job-related skills. In hindsight, however, Marsha feels that the
decision to drop out of high school and study specific vocational skills was
a poor one. Although she studied basic reading, writing, and math, and
she learned about different trades such as building maintenance and culi-
nary arts, she does not feel that she has anything to show for what she
knows.

> I felt that if I would have stayed there, I would have graduated, but
> then at that time my mother thought Job Corps was good for me
> by just being away, being up there, being upstate. But it's not that I
> didn't get nothing out of it, but I didn't come home with a diploma
> like a high school diploma or a GED or something. Now I have
> nothing.

She attributes her reading problem to the fact that she never attended the same school for very long, and therefore lacks a "proper" education. "I feel that I am very bright. I catch on very quick and learn very quick," Marsha says of herself. Prior to coming to the literacy program, Marsha says, "I wasn't really reading. It's just like I was reading around, reading songs, reading . . . not really having a main book and just sticking to that book in reading." Sometimes she would pick up a newspaper on the train left by other passengers. She would look over the articles and occasionally be surprised by how much she could understand. Similarly, Marsha liked to pick up the Bible and read from whatever page she opened to: "I would just sit there and try to read that page and try to understand it. . . . Whatever page I open up to I just start from there, whatever."

Before coming to LVNYC, Marsha attended a literacy program offered through a local college. She says it was a good program and she liked her teacher but it was closed suddenly without explanation. After taking a summer off, Marsha and her mother enrolled in LVNYC together. The two attend at different sites and Marsha doesn't know if her mother is still going to the program or not. At the time Marsha was interviewed for this study, she had been attending the program for about 8 months.

Life Inside the Program: "I Wish That I Could Fly like a Bird"

Marsha attends literacy classes two nights a week. One night her tutoring group focuses on reading, and on the second night they do more writing. Writing has provided Marsha a new tool for personal growth and insight and she says that this aspect of the program has been the most useful to her.

> When I first got here . . . I wrote about myself and what I want to do in life and everything and that was my first time ever you know really writing about myself because I never used to, you know, really sit down and write about myself. I'd just write about things, you know, but not really what I want to do at my life's time. You know so, that helped . . . and then they got me to start noticing myself by writing it out.

Marsha keeps a journal, which she carries back and forth between home and class. She explains that the journal entries are "my own words, my feelings about what I write about." Tutors at LVNYC encourage Marsha to focus her attention initially on expressing ideas rather than on getting the grammar and spelling right. Consequently, she leaves a blank space for troublesome words or phrases and returns to these later.

Journal writing means much more to Marsha than an exercise for learning grammar and spelling. Her journal has become a tool for deriving meaning from the dailiness of her life. It is one place where the ordinary and the spiritual are brought together. For example, an entry about racism, violence, and the role of police is followed by this entry posing central questions about human existence and life after death:

> How do people feel about life like when you die? What do you think about the other side? How do you feel about the other side because on this side is full of hate, hateful, racists, painful . . . it's like, everything. But on the other side, it's like full of love, happiness, joyness, you go through no pain, no problems, no nothing.

In another entry Marsha recorded events of her day including an opportunity that arose at her job. Through the writing she explored her feelings about this opportunity: "I'm going to go do it, but I really don't care too much about it." Marsha explained to her interviewer that her thoughts continued to evolve until she questioned how much control she really has over who she is and who she might become. She shared a later entry inspired by the event:

> Sometime I look up in the sky and I watch the birds. The clouds and the birds go by and sometime I wish that I could fly like a bird. And then I was saying, I wonder if it's God's choice to decide if we're human beings or what. Sometime we come out as a bird or a fly or an ant or anything. Is it His choice to decide what we should be in life? Who knows?

Marsha notices changes in herself since she has been attending the program. She does not, however, describe being able to read more words than before. She is not sure whether she picks up different types of reading material now than she would have in the past. Instead, she knows she is progressing because of the feeling she has of *wanting* to read more. Since she started writing in the program, she realizes that she can read her own writing with no problem but sometimes she can see the same words somewhere else and not recognize them. Another change she has experienced has to do with the way she uses writing now as a means for developing greater self-awareness.

> Because sometime you can notice yourself or even see yourself just by writing it out sometimes. And sometimes people walk around with a blindfold over their faces . . . don't even realize they're here.

> And by me . . . like they say you can express more out in writing
> and you know instead of actually sometimes saying it over the
> phone or talking or whatever.

Marsha does not explain her writing progress in terms of writing more now
than before, or writing with fewer errors. Marsha focuses on how she is
able to use writing now to deepen her understanding of herself and the
world.

Marsha lives by the maxim "Whatever you put in, that's what you
get out," and she wonders if the two nights a week she devotes to attending literacy classes are really enough. Although work and family obliga-
tions compete for her time and energy, she believes that inner discipline
and drive are the central issues affecting her progress: "It's all up to me as
to how much I want to put into it. . . . I know now that I can do it. I just
have to push myself more and stop saying it and do. . . . If I want to get
out there and get another job, really, I don't have a choice."

She does not want to end up like some of her friends who, she says,
"have all this knowledge, education, diplomas, and stuff. And they don't
do nothing with theirselves. Just stay home and watch stories." Marsha
also is aware that conditions within the program, such as tutor turnover,
impact her progress. One tutor that she became particularly close to recently left the program. Marsha experienced this change as a great loss
because

> me and her just started getting to know one another you know and
> sit down and talk about anything with each other. I can communi-
> cate, where before it was like I couldn't even communicate with
> anybody here because I just didn't feel, you know, feel opening . . .
> opening up to that person.

Life Outside the Program:
"Everywhere You Go . . . You Got to Read"

Long before entering the program, Marsha learned to adapt in some situations and to avoid other situations that would require her to engage in
unfamiliar literacy practices. She has chosen not to have a checking account, for instance, because she says that she wants to avoid the possibility that someone might steal her checkbook and write bad checks in her
name. Having never owed anybody anything, she feels that she does not
want to start now. This is the same reasoning that keeps her from acquir-
ing credit cards. Marsha does use a savings account, which she finds easy

to manage. She carries a small book with her that provides the spelling for numbers such as 100 or 1,000. When she needs to write out a number, she just looks it up in her book. Her savings account transactions are generally quite simple and predictable: Each time she writes the date, the amount of her transaction, and her account number on the deposit or withdrawal slip.

Marsha usually goes to restaurants where she is familiar with the menu items so ordering is not a problem. In a strange restaurant, she might simply ask if what she wants is served there. This works for her, but Marsha says that as a way of life, getting by without reading is hard. "It's hard . . . because it's like everywhere you go sometimes, you know, it's required that you got to read something to know what's going on."

Having worked at the bakery for three years, Marsha has mastered the tasks associated with serving customers and says that it is time for her to learn new skills. She feels she is ready to move up to a shift supervisor's position. In fact, she has already been given a lot of the responsibility of a shift supervisor, such as opening and closing the store each day and doing the cash-out. However, she has not been offered the salary or benefits that normally come with a supervisor's position. Instead, Marsha is told that she must first become certified through a company-sponsored training program. Her boss approved her participation in the 7-week course and also offered to help her with the course reading if necessary.

The course, which meets for 3 hours each week, focuses on daily procedures that supervisors need to know such as filling out service reports and adhering to health and safety regulations. Marsha does not seem bothered by the large amount of reading required in the course—about 100 or so typed pages—because the instructor and her supervisor help by discussing the material with her. Moreover, she relies a lot on what she learned through daily experience. In fact, she reveals to her interviewer, "I haven't really read any of this stuff because I know the majority of stuff that's in here." Although Marsha says that she could read most of the materials on her own if she wanted to, she says that she would not have even considered taking the course if the instructor and her supervisor had not both agreed to help her with literacy if needed.

Relationships and Social Support: "It's Like Everybody's Doing Their Own Separate Things"

Marsha is the only one among the five children in her family without a high school diploma. She fantasizes about coming home to her mother one day and saying, "Here is my diploma. Hang it up on the wall!" Her brothers and sisters are aware that she attends a literacy program but they don't know much about what she is actually learning in the program or the significance this learning holds for Marsha. For instance, the brother and sister with whom she lives have no idea about all the writing she is doing. Marsha says that the three of them, although they live together, really don't interact with one another very much. "When I come in I just like to, you know, be by myself, whatever, and sometime they don't even be home. . . . It's like everybody is doing their own separate things." What this means for Marsha, then, is that no one in her home serves to encourage or support her efforts. Marsha does share her writing with one younger sister who lives with their mother. Every now and then she will ask the sister to respond to something she has written or to help her with a piece in progress. Occasionally, she might ask this sister for help with other reading and writing practices, such as filling out a form.

It becomes clear listening to Marsha that some of her family and friends are "in" and others are "out" when it comes to being privy to her reading problem. The way that Marsha shares her writing with one particular sister but not with her mother or her other siblings is one example of this. Marsha explains how she has also sought help with her reading from one boyfriend in the past. However, she has this to say about her current boyfriend:

> I'm not that open with him with my problem with reading and writing. Like with [my old boyfriend] he understood. You know he helped me. We sat down to read, trying to read and write this and that. With [my current boyfriend] it's like different. I'm not going to never say that he would never sit down and do these things with me but I don't think I would want him to.

At work, Marsha will go to her supervisor for help with reading or writing practices but she does not seek help from co-workers, who remain, as far as she knows, unaware of her problem.

These stories reflect established patterns in Marsha's relationships. Other relationships in Marsha's life have been changing as her life-style has changed. She explains,

> I see a lot of my friends doing the same old things year after year and I'm not into that really no more. I used to get high, go to parties, you know, do all those things, but now my life has changed. . . . I stay really more to myself than with my friends . . . and now I feel good about myself. . . . I mean, they can't do anything that's going to really make me happy. We're still friends, but

it's just that we not that close as we used to be by hanging around each other everyday. . . . I can't let nothing stop me. . . . They even noticed that where I don't be around them no more. I don't do the things that they do.

At the same time that she feels herself drifting away from old friends, Marsha finds herself becoming busier. Taking care of her own needs is time-consuming, she has discovered. She explains, "I have a lot of stuff to do really to take care of . . . because I'm paying my own insurance, paying my telephone bill. I buy my own clothes, you know, and whatever I need, you know, I do for myself. . . . I don't ask anybody for nothing. And there's always somebody needs something. If I have it, I will give it." Marsha also joined a women's gym and has begun working out regularly. Despite these life-style changes and shifts in her relationships, old friends are not entirely gone from Marsha's life.

Marsha's interviewer asked her how coming to the literacy program might have contributed to the changes she has recently undergone. Without hesitating, Marsha explained that it was the writing she has been doing that helped her make changes in her life: "Because like I said, it got me to realize what I really want by—by me just writing out so much. So much of feelings and by me coming here like I said. This is just the beginning by me writing out my feelings."

Attending the program is a means to an end for Marsha. She looks forward to the day that literacy problems will not be an issue for her. And among the scenarios she plays out in her mind is this one—her final exit from the program.

Say the graduation day . . . you have to make a speech and here I'm writing out this speech that I must read in front of a thousand people, whatever, you know. I would love to be able to just read about my life and how did I grow up and how did I struggle to be able to learn how to read and write. And to get up on the stage and to read this you know. I would love to do something like that.

3

Don: "Keep Going for Your Goal in Life"

Don is an African-American man, about 25 years old, single, unemployed, and living with his mother in New York City at the time of these interviews. As far as he knows, his father died before he was born. Don grew up the youngest of nine children. His brothers, he said, "would play my daddy . . . you know, like try to boss me around and make me go upstairs and what not." His mother, who raised the children alone, often had trouble getting clothes for everyone, so Don had to wear clothes borrowed from friends and hand-me-downs from his brothers and sisters. A particularly painful memory for Don is not attending his sixth-grade graduation because he didn't have a suit to wear. He says he always felt that he had less than other children and that this made him feel mad. Adding insult to injury, other children used to tease him because he had a speech problem. "I didn't have no other friends," says Don, "so . . . I was stuck with them." According to Don's mother, he was always shy around other children and didn't make many friends at school.

Prior Schooling Experiences: "They Thought We Was Crazy"

When Don was in elementary school, his mother was told that he was slightly retarded and that he needed to be placed in special education classes. Don says his mother went along with this plan because she believed that school personnel had his best interests in mind. He, on the other hand, believes that he was placed in special education for the convenience of teachers: "I was slow and everybody else would be finished writing the words down and I still be like half-way finished." Don feels that he didn't really need to be in special education, "because in time I would have, you know, got fast or faster if I would have stayed in the normal class." He painfully remembers how he hated to stand in line in the school hallway with his special education classmates. He recalls, "other kids come by and say 'retarded kids' like they thought we was crazy."

Don feels his teachers pushed him along, passing him at each level just so he could ultimately finish school. He did not take issue with this because he really wanted to get out and get a job and "make some money." However, now he feels that most of his teachers were not really helping him. He can remember times when, in fact, they embarrassed him by making him read out loud even though he expressly asked them not to:

> You know they like try to embarrass me in front of the other students because I'd tell them before going to class, I'd say I can't really read so don't ask me to really read because I can't. I don't know that word . . . and he'd ask me any old way, you know . . . and the kids would start laughing at me . . . so sometimes I didn't go to certain classes.

There were other times when he felt that teachers violated his trust. For instance, one time Don asked one teacher to explain to another teacher that he could not read. He trusted that this conversation would result in his not being asked to read in front of the other students. When he was asked to read in class, Don remembers feeling shocked and let down by the teachers; he felt he could not rely on them to protect him. When he was in the ninth grade, a teacher told Don that she could not really take time out to help him because it would not be fair to the other students, so he recalls that he "just sat there" and looked at his papers after telling her that he understood.

Don avoided embarrassing situations by not attending certain classes. He says he would walk the halls or go to the gym and lift weights. He was less intimidated by threats of being reported to the principal than he was by facing the embarrassment he felt when asked to read out loud in front of others.

Don says that his best friend from high school, Kevin, had doubts about Don's ability to read but never confronted him about it. Even as adults, the subject has never come up. Don says, "He went along with it as I went along with it. . . . He never asked me and I never told him and he still don't know." Don remembers occasions with Kevin when he pretended to read. For instance, one time Kevin had a letter from a girlfriend that he wanted to share with Don.

> And so I had to pretend that I knew what the letter said. He's saying "Yes, she really love me," and I said "Uh huh, uh huh." . . . So that was hard because not that he would laugh at me or make fun but just that I was scared. I didn't want to take that chance.

An older sister would often help Don with reading practices when he was growing up. For example, Don says that he was afraid to travel on the train for fear of getting lost and not being able to follow the directions that other people gave him; so his sister would go with him. She also helped him fill out forms and read things to him when necessary. Also, Don says his mother would always do everything for him. This upset some siblings who thought that Don should do more for himself—not only for his own good but so that their mother would not have the extra burden of caring for a grown son.

> My mother like did everything for me and she spoiled me seems like and you know I don't know why she did it but she did. I can't change the way that I am so a lot of people get mad. Like my sisters and brothers get mad. I say, it ain't my fault. If I ask my mother to keep this for me or fix this for me or whatever time I come in the house or it's late and I say, "Ma I want to eat," she get up and heat up the food for me. Things like that. And she wouldn't do it for them so they would be mad.

In his late teens, Don attended a job training and counseling program for about two years. Coincidentally, this was a time in Don's life when he felt deeply depressed and even considered killing himself. He felt that he was different from the other participants who attended the job training program, many of whom were physically disabled and in wheelchairs. He says his problem was different in that he "only struggled with his reading." He observed that many attending this program never actually got jobs.

Don developed an important relationship with his counselor in this program.

> For awhile he was telling me his problems and in a way that would make me feel good in that I'm younger and he's older and a lot of older people telling me their problems makes me feel good, makes me feel good about myself that, you know, they can talk to me instead of talking to someone older. Saying, "Don, you're a real good person, you know. You smart and you know you got brains on you and what not. You know, keep going for your goal in life."

These words of encouragement appear to have had a powerful impact on Don's sense of self and thoughts of ending his life dissipated.

Don recalls that he spent most of his time sitting at home watching television during the few years prior to entering an adult literacy program for the first time: "I wouldn't go outside. You know, I wouldn't be with nobody. I would just stay in the house." Don says he couldn't work be-cause he needed a high school diploma and he says that "nobody would want me to work for them." He also says that his mother received advice and criticism from her friends. For instance, Don recalls people saying to his mother,

> "Why you do this to your son? Why don't you get him help? He's 21 years old. Now he's getting older and he going to need money in his life and what not." She was like saying she tried and that, you know, she was trying. I was telling her, "Don't cry and it's not your fault."

Don often refers to being mad and describes himself as a victim: "I can't change the way that I am." Yet, he is working to change the way that he is and he can, in fact, describe real change.

Life Inside the Program: "I'm Just Going to Sit There and Be Mad"

Don's mother located the literacy program and took him there the first time. She also told him exactly how to travel on the train so that he could go there on his own the next time. He says, "I was awfully scared and wanted her to come with me down there."

When asked what he'd like to get out of the program, Don says, "I just want to be able to read a little better where I could read a book or, you know, I do things on my own and not have to ask people to help me read all the time." He wants to do things the way others do them. He wants to be independent. When he gets to that point, he says he will tell his friends about his reading problems.

As Don describes his experience with the instructional program at LVNYC, it becomes apparent that both predictability and control are im-portant to him. For example, when the interviewer asked Don if he might have chosen among several different class sites, he says,

> Yeah, but I got used to my tutor so I didn't want to try another program. And, I didn't want to be traveling a lot. I learned my way getting here so I didn't want to try it to do something new. Give this one a chance. If it really don't work out for me, then I try another one.

Don has particular notions about the tutors with whom he works. He describes how one tutor seems to feel sorry for people who are unable to read. "It's like she's feeling guilty in a way that, you know, she got to do this. But it's like she don't really have to do this because everybody ain't cut out to do it." Don explains how another tutor who seems "really into it" will not, nevertheless, help him the way he wants to be helped.

Don, as well as the tutors, become accustomed to and comfortable with particular teaching strategies. Both find change difficult. Shortly after he started the program, one of his two tutors left to go back to school and Don felt angry. He felt close to her and had become used to her teaching style. As Don explains it, "I've been with my other tutor and like it's hard to change and do something else when you been doing something different for a long time."

Tutors come and go regularly. Some stand out in Don's mind:

> One was, she was so nice and sweet and what not and it's just that she couldn't do it because she was so sensitive and she was, you know, she wouldn't say nothing and she was always on your side and you know I wanted her to be more firm, more out with it, you know, more "into" it. She was like real quiet and what not. And she didn't really . . . it's like in a way she didn't really know what she was doing but she wanted to. You know she really wanted to do it. But she didn't know how.

A good teacher, according to Don, is someone who is consistently present and reliable and who cares for him as a unique individual. He senses that a good teacher works *for* him and enjoys the work. A good teacher is firm with him, supportive, and confident in his or her ability to teach him. By firm, Don says, "I need someone who's not going to constantly let me have my way all the time. It's like I want someone to be a little more demanding." He goes on to say, "I want them to care if I do it or if I don't do it." He remembers public school teachers who would say to him, "You do the work or don't do it . . . I don't care. You're the one who has to learn." Such teachers, he says, made him feel worse about himself. A good teacher, according to Don, is responsive to his requests for particular kinds of assistance. A good teacher matches his or her teaching style to Don's learning style. He prefers that teachers spend a lot of one-on-one time with him and believes that he learns faster this way. When a teacher shows that she is really trying to help, Don says this makes him want to try harder to help himself. Don says that his progress is interrupted whenever one of the teachers to whom he is accustomed leaves. He says, "I feel myself dropping, dropping, dropping all the way back down where I started from."

When Don feels dissatisfied with how things are going for him in the program, he describes resistance behavior similar to that exhibited during his early schooling.

Sometimes I haven't been coming because I didn't like the group and one of them I don't like. It wasn't nearly so much of the group, it was like of the tutors. But [then] like I say I'm going to come. I'm just going to sit there and be mad and then they'll ask me why I'm mad. And I tell her, "Because you're not helping me."

When asked if he has shared his concerns with the center director, Don says that he did but that generally he does not like to hurt anyone's feelings. He is worried that the tutors will think "he just has to have his way" whereas from his perspective he's trying to convey what he's learned through experience about the reading process and what he believes about teaching/learning strategies that work best for him.

Don speaks specifically about the kind of assistance he wants from his tutor:

Like if I don't know this word in this book I prefer you to tell me instead of letting me beat my brains out trying to figure out what it is because I'm not going to know what it is because I'm not good with the sounds.

He explains that tutors can make him feel comfortable with a book when they help him with the words. As the conversation continues, Don says that it is not so much that he cannot guess a lot of words correctly, but rather that he's not as *accustomed* to having to do a lot of guessing. He feels that the tutors ought to help him the way he wants to be helped: "So [when] they do it the way they want it to be done, they not really helping you too much. And that's when sometimes I don't like to come, and I don't want to be bothered. See with my old group, they always helped me."

Don has mixed feelings about his tutoring group. Sometimes he feels that he doesn't get enough attention from his group. He senses that this is the case for others, too. He has observed that sometimes students do not return the next day after not getting the help they need from tutors. Even though this is the same strategy that Don has used in the past, he says of another group member, "He's just given up . . . that's not going to help. [He'll] be right back where he started from."

Don says he has become friends with some of the people in his group, but the friendships do not extend outside the program and don't seem like other "real" friendships.

It's like we friends but we don't really talk or conversate about nothing, like once in awhile we might ask for each other's help you know, something like that. . . . It's like I don't feel like they my friends. It's just that they're some people that I'm working with.

Life Outside the Program: "I Used to Feel like I Was Stupid"

Don dreams of improving his literacy abilities and having a "nice city job" and his own place. He wants to be able to read restaurant menus and letters. Don says that he wanted to be a police officer when he was a child, but now he says, "I just want to be happy and be able to live and enjoy my life. So, I'll do the things that I want to do."

Since coming to LVNYC, Don, his mother, and his sister can describe several changes related to his literacy practices, his personal qualities, and his self-concept. In class he learned how to read some of the signs that help him get to and from the program on the subway. He says he depends on himself more now and less on others generally in his life, not just in relation to literacy practices. For instance, he says he irons his own clothes now and cooks more for himself.

Don has tried new practices since entering the program and found out that they are not as difficult as he had imagined. He got his own telephone, for example, and asked his sister to help him figure out the bill. He also learned how to buy a money order. He talks about other things he wants to accomplish such as understanding his electric bill. He says he is now doing a lot of things that everyone else does. He attributes this to the program and says that if it were not for the program he would "probably still be in the house doing nothing." He says he is now trying to "do different things to see could I do it."

Don's sister Yvette confirms the changes Don describes in himself. She says:

> He really tries and tries to do more, not sitting around doing nothing. He tries to do a lot of things to keep busy and help hisself. . . . He does more on his own like write, filling out stuff, before he would just give it to somebody and let them do it for him, but he will do it hisself now.

Yvette says that Don is not as embarrassed as he used to be about showing others what he has written. She thinks that he is not as afraid as he used to be of how others might react to his reading and writing problems. Both Don's mother and Yvette talk about how Don uses the subway now more often and with greater confidence. They also agree that he seems less shy around other people. His mother thinks that the classes make him feel a little more secure with himself and that this accounts for changes in his behavior and routines.

Don says that he used to be scared to go grocery shopping because he did not think that he could count his money correctly. He would have someone shop with him or he would take the receipt and his change back home and have someone check it for him. Don says he knows what to buy from going with his mother. He recognizes things in the grocery store from seeing them all the time and because he always buys the same things. If he wants something new, his mother tells him the name and he tries to remember it. Mostly he just remembers the way things look, such as the color of the package and the sound of the first letter.

Don describes his life prior to coming to the program this way:

> I felt like I couldn't really do nothing and my mother and my sisters they always helped me. And, I never really went outside. I stayed in the house and watched TV and I really had no friends and really nothing to do and I didn't want to meet nobody or have any friends because I couldn't read and they could so I just stayed in the house all the time. I never went out to visit no family or anybody like that because I wouldn't know how to get there and if I had to take the train, I'd say forget it, won't go. Or I'd wait until one of them go . . . or I take a cab.

Don says that he wants to become more independent from his mother and siblings, but he also reveals some of the difficulties he encounters with this goal. For example, Don explained to an interviewer how he pretends to be less competent than he really is, sometimes. This is to avoid changes in his relationships and life-style. Don is aware that changes in his literacy practices will be accompanied by changes in the way he and others relate to one another.

> Sometime if I knew how to do it, I would act like I couldn't do it. Like I would act like I don't know how to do that. And they would like come with me or show me. . . . Because I never really used to do things on my own. I always have someone there with me or someone coming with me or someone there. It's like when you move out and you get your own place, it's like you're not used to being by yourself. . . . I'm always used to having someone there who I could depend on.

Don says he does not write much when he is home. Brothers, sisters, nieces, and nephews come and go through his house; it is noisy, and he does not want them to see him working on his lessons. Don also finds it difficult to get help at home; he describes the frustration that both he and his sister experience when she tries to help him: "She'll like yell, you know, 'Sound it out! Just say the word!' . . . A lot of the time, she think it's like easy. But trying to tell someone who know how to read to someone who don't know how to read that it's easy, it's not." Sometimes Don asks for help from his mother. He might ask her the meaning of a word that he's heard on television or how to spell something. He's more likely, however, to save his questions and his writing practice for his time inside the program.

The family members feel that relationships among them haven't changed since Don began making progress in his reading and writing. However, Don sees that his friendships seem to be shifting. He says that he and his old friends have started to "go their different ways" because he does not want any of them to ask him about his classes. He has told them that the classes are related to learning the computer.

The deep sense of shame that has persisted throughout Don's life continues despite progress made in the program. He says, "I'm not afraid to get on the train now or get on the bus. I know my way a little bit. I'm not scared or frightened. But the . . . one thing I'm still kind of scared of is I don't tell nobody that I can't read but it's like certain people I want to tell but I just can't tell them." At another point in the interview he explains, "I'm just so scared, I'm so embarrassed, too ashamed of it. It's hard for me to get out of that." Don says,

> I always thought I couldn't read nothing. And I didn't know no words. So I always felt like I was a dummy. And I didn't want to be with nobody or see nobody because I used to feel like I was stupid, and nobody likes me and I don't want to be bothered with nobody.

Don continues:

> Sometime I want to talk to [certain women] but I can't because I don't want them to get too close to me because I don't want them to know that I can't read. And I feel that they might, you know, make fun. And then when I decide to get close, it's too late. They got a boyfriend, they having a baby already and I'm missing out. Gosh! . . . It's like I think they going to make fun or they don't want no guy who can't read or something like that.

Don has never told any of his friends outside the program that he can't read. He can describe many examples of bluffing his way through situations alongside friends, such as ordering in restaurants or "reading" flyers that announce parties or musical events. He says he wishes that his friends would just come out and say something about his reading problem so that he wouldn't have to tell them himself: "I'm just waiting for them to say

'You can't read and I'm not going to make fun of you. I'm your friend and you could tell me.' They ain't never came out and said nothing like that."

Don is worried that if he tells his friends, the conversation might lead to a breakup of a friendship. He wants to be assured by his friends that they will still like him. Also, he would like to be certain that his friends won't treat him differently because of his reading problem. He wants them to joke around with him and treat him like anybody else—not like someone with a learning problem. He does not want them to be careful of what they say around him for fear of hurting his feelings. Don believes that his friends would feel hurt also if they said anything that might *knowingly* embarrass him. He says that he does not want them to experience awkwardness around him because of his problem so he tries to shield them from it. He feels his relationships are somehow more genuine this way. What they say to him might cause him embarrassment anyway but his friends need not know this and are thus spared some discomfort.

4

Ann: "I Just Didn't
Want to Make Trouble"

Ann grew up in rural southwest Virginia during the 1930s. Her father, like many African Americans in the area at that time, was a field worker and moved the family from one farm to another as work became available. Depending on where they were living, Ann and her sisters walked as far as four miles to school. Sometimes they got to school only because the teacher stopped by in the morning to offer them a ride. More often than not, however, Ann and her sisters were not allowed to go to school even if they had the means to get there. "You didn't need it on the farm" is what Ann remembers her father saying about education. Based on his ability to count, Ann always assumed that her father had received at least some education. Even so, he did not think that education particularly mattered for his daughters. He used to say that if "he could make it then we could make it," Ann remembers. When interviewed for this study, Ann was 65, recently retired, and a great-grandmother living in New York City. Despite the passing of time, she held resentment toward her father. According to Ann, it "seemed like he didn't try to make a way for us. . . . And like today, my sister . . . he dead God bless him . . . she hates him today for that."

Prior Schooling: "I Just Stopped"

At 16, Ann moved to Baltimore, where she had a few cousins and friends. Her intent was to finish high school there but she quickly discovered that she was far behind the other students. Also, her new class had 20 students and only one teacher. It was hard for her to follow everything that the teacher wrote on the blackboard and she felt that she never received the extra assistance needed in order to catch up with the other students. Regardless of what she encountered as a new student trying to make up for lost time, the real truth, she believes, is that she just quit learning. "I had men and boys in my mind so I just stopped." Still a teenager, Ann quit high school, married, and started a family. In addition to raising three children, she worked 40 years in factory production.

Throughout most of her adult life, Ann was resigned to the notion that her own education was essentially an opportunity lost. She recognized but avoided subsequent opportunities to develop her literacy ability, not wanting to experience the embarrassment that had become part and parcel of her reading and writing difficulty. To illustrate this, Ann recalled her experience as a parent trying to help her son with schoolwork. During a homework session when he was about 11 years old, Ann's son realized that his mother couldn't read. She remembers him saying to her, "Mommy, I'll help you." But Ann didn't take the opportunity. She explains, "I was too embarrassed, you know. But [he] would have helped me. I could have learned right along with him."

Ann first learned about Literacy Volunteers of New York City (LVNYC) on television when she was 62 years old. Coincidentally, her two sisters back in Virginia had become involved in a literacy program at about that same time. More significantly, Ann's friend Felicia, who had been trying to find a home tutor for Ann, began to encourage Ann to attend LVNYC. Ann refers to Felicia as her "goddaughter." Felicia's husband was attending LVNYC, and Felicia gave the phone number to Ann. However, Ann says, "I just kept putting it off. . . . I kept saying I'm not ready for this. But all the time I wanted this, you know."

Felicia was a vital source of assistance, as Ann explains: "She do a lot of things for me. Like she was taking me shopping and stuff, you know, with the car. She even carried me down South to see my mother and them, I think about three years ago." When Ann put off calling LVNYC, Felicia threatened to stop helping her; eventually, Felicia agreed to make the initial phone call and arrange Ann's first meeting with the program staff. Felicia also agreed to drive Ann to the classes each week if necessary. As it turned out, Ann was able to walk to a program offered near her apartment in Brooklyn. At the time she was interviewed for this study, Ann had been attending the program for three years.

Life Inside the Program: "There Are So Many Words That I'm Missing"

Ann rarely used to talk to anyone about her reading difficulty. Furthermore, before entering the literacy program, she never considered that there might be other adults who had similar problems. Having lived most of her life feeling uniquely afflicted, Ann was relieved to meet others like herself:

I was so embarrassed, feeling so bad about it because I never talked
about it to other people, you know, and [I was] always in the
closet. When I came here I was so shocked to see so many young
people out here with the same thing. You can't talk about me, I
can't talk about you. We are all here for the same thing and that's
why I feel so comfortable.

When she first started the program, Ann was tested to determine her
reading level and then assigned to a tutor. Initially, she and one other student shared a tutor. Soon, however, they were joined by four or five more
students and a second tutor. As Ann gained experience as an adult
student, she accumulated ways to understand and explain her reading
progress. Instructional programs for adults are organized differently than
schools, she explains. "Some kids go to school 20 years . . . 9 months a year
for 6 hours a day." LVNYC offers Ann instruction only two hours a day,
two days a week. She says that learning to read at this pace may take a
long time. As she puts its, it may take "two years, three years, four years
for me to get out of here." From another perspective, Ann believes that
her "brain" can hold only so much information. This belief affords her an
explanation for why the responsibilities of adulthood seem to interfere with
her ability to retain what she learns in the program.

See, we got so much in our minds, so much in our brains raising
children, getting married, making a living and all of that. It's so
hard to put anything else in there because it's so hard for me to
hold things. . . . I can't concentrate on my brain enough to hold it
in. You know when you're young you can just keep it in and spell
it and you know [it]. . . . I'm trying to learn this and trying to cook
dinner. I'm trying to shop. All that's in my mind you know. It's too
much.

Sometimes Ann attends the program more regularly than other times.
She notices that her attendance affects the pace of her learning. She re-
marked on a few occasions to her interviewer that she "would have been
further in this but I slacked off myself. . . . I have to get back in the speed
because I think I should have been more advanced than I am, but I slacked
up myself." These remarks reveal a third way that Ann understands her
progress, this time as it relates to her drive and self-discipline.

On any given day, Ann's tutoring group might work with a newspaper designed especially for new readers. Everyone takes a turn reading out
loud. Then group members talk about what they have read and how they
feel about it. They work together by helping one another with difficult

words. If Ann knows a word that someone else doesn't, for instance, she will just say it out loud.

Ann measures her need for learning in terms of "words." There are words she knows, and words she doesn't know. She speaks of words that others know, and of words that she needs to know. To Ann, reading is recognizing individual words and knowing how to spell them without having to ask for help. Also, for Ann, the learning process is marked by a beginning and an end. She says, "I want to start from the beginning because there are so many words that I'm missing." Ann will know that she has reached the end of her studies when she can read a newspaper headline—not because this is necessarily a personal goal she set for herself, but because she has somehow gotten the idea that the program requires all students to read the newspaper before they leave the program. Stating her goals in a more personalized way, Ann wants to be able to pick up a book and "just read it and read it and read it." She also looks forward to being able to write a letter when she feels like it without having to ask anyone for help with spelling.

Because of the way Ann understands the process of learning to read, it makes sense to her that her tutors would tell her the words she doesn't know as she encounters them. She says that learning a new word this way is encouraging. During silent reading, however, tutors at LVNYC encourage focus on meaning rather than on decoding discrete words. They ask students to finish reading their selection before receiving help. In the meantime, students focus on figuring out troublesome words based on the context of the passage. According to Ann, she gets "disgusted" when she has to sit for 20 minutes or an hour waiting for someone to help her with a word. She explains, "You don't know what it is, you keep sitting there looking at that word. Tell me this word then I can go onto the next word. It makes a big difference. People don't realize that." Ann experiences similar frustration when it comes to writing:

> You can't tell me to start writing a letter here and I don't know how to spell "dear." So, you got to tell me how to spell it. "Just figure out how it should go." That's what they said. I said I can't figure how it should go. If I know that I would stay home and do it, right?

"They're getting me to work, that's for sure," Ann says about her tutors. She is referring to the fact that the tutors want Ann to try and write "a little something" every day and to "read something long." Ann has set an additional personal goal for herself, which is to "learn two new words" each day so that maybe writing will become easier for her. She explained the difficulty she experiences trying to write: "It's a lot of little words I can't spell without looking at them. But I done looked at them a lot and when I do see them I know what it is. And I am looking at it, I can spell it. But to close the book and spell it, I find it hard."

Ann struggles with learning to spell even short words correctly but she enjoys the techniques her tutors use to try to and help her. She likes her tutors' use of large newsprint paper to demonstrate writing, which is then posted on the walls. She also likes the use of the blackboard. Ann explains that her tutors "go over and over" everything, explaining patiently and breaking tasks down into smaller steps that Ann finds comfortable.

Ann thinks of her tutoring group as a "nice group"; the members are friendly to one another and they often talk with each other about personal things in addition to reading. "Like me and Dora," Ann explains, "We talk about numbers a lot. [We] play numbers, you know . . . so it's relaxing." Through her years of work experience she has learned that "on the job, you can talk to somebody once in awhile and say something and smile. The work goes better." Likewise, she values the informal conversation that goes on in her tutoring group. It contributes to her sense of confidence and bolsters her willingness to try new things. Ann feels that if she's not comfortable with the members of her group, it's like "exposing yourself . . . and it's not too good." In addition to the friendly rapport that has developed among members of her group, she likes the way everyone works interdependently. "It's like you're helping each other," Ann says. "Like if you get hung up on a sentence . . . I'll say it, and that keeps them going before the tutor say it. It helps a lot."

Ann has had the opportunity to work with a few different tutors since she started the program and she's decided that "the spirit have to agree with them. . . . If the spirit don't agree . . . it's no good." She readily compares the personalities and teaching styles of the various tutors she has worked with. Around one tutor in particular, Ann experienced a lot of stress because, as she says:

> It seemed like I wasn't getting no place. She kept me just reading. She'd get a book or something and she'd tell me to read something else and mark it and just, you know, but I'm going crazy. I said I can sit at home and do this. Figure out what that next word is. It was too much, I couldn't deal with it.

Ann contrasts this tutor with another who "wouldn't only answer the question, but most of the time he explained what it meant. And sometime he would go and get the dictionary to let you know the difference between this and that." This is the tutoring approach she describes as most beneficial.

When Ann feels that she's not moving ahead she is inclined to stop attending the program for periods of time. As she describes herself, she has never been the kind of program participant who speaks out about what she likes and what she doesn't like in the way of instruction. This may have to do with the fact that Ann, like others who attend the program, is aware that the tutors are volunteers. Students don't always think it is within their right to criticize people who are already giving their time and "doing the best they can." The last time she felt a lot of frustration over the way things were going with her tutor, Ann remembers, "I just didn't want to make trouble. I didn't want to say nothing because . . . sometimes she . . . don't get me wrong, she was a nice person, but I don't know . . . I don't think she really know how to do it." Ann wasn't at peace with her decision to stay silent, however. She admits, "That's what got me disgusted, I didn't say nothing . . . I couldn't say nothing because she was a nice person, you know."

Life Outside the Program: "I Would Always Stay in the Background"

When Ann retired from her job after 40 years, she felt like a load had been lifted from her shoulders. For all those years she had worked to hide her literacy problem from co-workers and supervisors:

> It's fortunate, I never got a position that I had to do a lot of writing. And when a position would come up for me to take it, because I was the seniorest, I refused it . . . I was afraid it would be reading and writing and I couldn't do it so I would always stay in the background and let somebody else take it. . . . All that burden down on you. . . . I'm glad the hard stuff is over.

Her job did require some counting because at the end of the day she had to "tell a machine" how much work she had produced. Ann describes handling this aspect of the work with relative comfort. She would keep a running count in her head all day rather than make notes to herself. Sometimes she admits pretending that she was in too big of a hurry to do the daily count. "Come pick this for me, girl, I'm in a hurry," Ann would say to one of her co-workers in order to avoid the counting process. "She'd say, 'Oh Ann' . . . then she'd do it."

Ann never makes a grocery list. She memorizes what she needs to buy and she looks at the pictures on food labels to help her decide if she is buying the right item. In other cases, she is familiar with the package design of common items so she doesn't have to worry about shopping mistakes. Recently, Ann's grandson came to live with her and he doesn't eat pork. This dietary restriction has posed a new challenge for Ann because it forces her to read the word "pork" on food labels. She says, "Now I really have to look at [the label]. I really have to watch what I'm buying. . . . I catch myself you know and sometime I go to grab something and it has pork in it. And I have to look at it and take it back." Being in the program has helped to increase Ann's level of confidence as she shops:

> I find myself comfortable now looking at the labels. I used to wonder and say what? and really study you know and stumble over the labels . . . for the pork and stuff . . . what it was made of and all that stuff. And now I can really understand more and I just [am] more comfortable doing that. I really watch the labels now, you know.

Ann's tutors have encouraged her to try making a grocery list but Ann is not persuaded by the idea that a shopping list might make her life easier. She has learned over the years that she can manage the list in her head well enough. She says, for instance, "I don't care if I get $100 for groceries. I don't make the list." She can, however, imagine that a shopping list might make for a good spelling exercise. And so, she says, "I'm going to get into that."

When asked about the kinds of reading and writing she does at home, Ann responds with the language of schooling. "That's my problem, I don't do it. If I study more at home and write, I would be more advanced. " She spends most of her time watching television and she says, "It's kind of hard for me to write and watch TV, too, you know." She says,

> Sometime I don't do it all day . . . pick up a pencil all day. But I will read something, you know, a little something. But not writing everyday like I should. And that's not good because they tell you to write something every day or read. So I know that's not what I'm supposed to do. I should do more. I say "after this story, after this story," and you know, that's it.

When Ann is at home and she comes across a word she does not know, she will write it down on a scrap of paper and then take it to her next tutoring session. "But," she says emphatically, "I won't ask nobody at home." Ann tries to understand the reason behind this:

> I don't know why really, I just can't do it. I feel shame or something. I don't know, I guess [it's] just me. . . . I just go on and

stumble over it or either write it down until I come here and then ask what it is. . . . I don't want to figure it out. That's why I come here.

Old Relationships and New Practices:
"Coming Out of the Closet, They Call It"

Ann observes that her relationships have changed a little bit as her independence around literacy tasks has increased. Since becoming involved in the program, she feels her relationships with family, and friends like Felicia, are getting "better and better." She reports that she is now able to read some letters and other items received in the mail. "That really took a burden off me. It makes me happy, it makes me feel good. . . . It really makes a big difference," she says. She also talks about reading short articles in a newspaper she subscribes to, called *The Big Red*. "Two years ago, I couldn't even do this," she shares excitedly.

Ann's children are supportive of her participation in LVNYC and they share the excitement she feels around her progress. She says that her son is "proud of me now that I'm going to school . . . because I'm going to school and getting better than I was." Ann feels that her relationship with her daughter has changed somewhat since she has been in the program because she no longer has to ask her to help with many "minor things." Her daughter had been the one in the family to handle all the banking, fill out forms when necessary, and pay the bills. Ann says "Thank God for that," but now Ann is able to fill out parts of some forms, at least. Ann is unclear about just how much of the family paperwork she has taken on herself, but every time she does not have to ask for assistance, she feels like she is relieved of a burden.

5

Maria: "I Don't Quit Easily"

Maria, a Hispanic woman in her early 30s, has been married to Jesus for more than 15 years. Together they are raising three children of their own along with a niece and a nephew who can no longer be cared for by Maria's sister. The family lives in an apartment above a converted storefront in Manhattan that once served as a church. Jesus ministered there until the medication he takes for asthma began to leave him disoriented and forgetful. Now he works a night job and Maria is working during the day as an aide in a neighborhood child care center.

Throughout Maria and Jesus' apartment, books spill from the milk crates that serve as shelves. In the living room games like Scrabble and Monopoly lie among many magazines. The family often reads books together. They especially like Agatha Christie murder mysteries and they take turns reading out loud to one another, stopping from time to time to guess who committed the murder. Maria has a strategy for encouraging reading within the family. She says, "I decided to take the *Reader's Digest* to the bathroom. Everybody loves to sit down in the bathroom and read. Since I've been doing that everybody is saying 'Ah, did you read this story in the *Reader's Digest*?'" Word games are also a favorite at Maria and Jesus' house. One time, Jesus says, they were playing a game with anagrams before he had to leave for work. "I came back from work and [Maria] was still working on the same word that I had left her with. Everybody was taking a turn."

Maria and Jesus intentionally provide a home environment for their children that centers around reading. Before the first child was even born, and long before Maria entered her first adult literacy program, she and Jesus bought "a whole milk crate full of books." Jesus remarks, "And we didn't even know if we were going to have any children." Remembering her own difficulties learning to read as a child, Maria wants to parent differently than her own mother and father:

> Sometimes I feel like I wish my parents would have been more
> understanding because they really . . . didn't really help me at all.

Not even with my reading. [Now] I try to see what's the problem and how can I help it. How can I help the child.

Maria didn't always enjoy reading and writing at home. There was a time when she avoided family activities requiring literacy practices. Her daughter remembers:

When I used to read books I used to say, "Oh, Mom, read this one." And she's like, "No, I can't read because my parents never taught me how to read or nothing." . . . Every time we used to ask her [to play word games] she'd say "Oh, I don't want to play," because she didn't know.

Maria described what she felt inside when faced with a reading or writing task:

I get scared. Sometimes I feel like crying when I write something and I don't know how to do it. And like I get hurt because I want to write something and say I want to write [Jesus] a letter. I don't know how to do it. I don't know how to express it. One time in church we had our couples' day and we were supposed to write something to our husbands. I never did it because I didn't know how to write it. The lady told me, "You could just tell him," and I didn't do that either.

Maria also avoided situations outside the home that could draw attention to her reading problem. When she first heard about a job opening at the day care center where she currently works, for instance, she waited two months to follow up on it. She explains, "I was scared. I didn't know if I could handle . . . you know. Because I know if you work in a day care center you got to do a lot of reading and writing and I was always scared to take that chance."

Early Schooling: "I Can't Read. Can You Help Me Out?"

Maria attributes her reading difficulty to a "mixture of a lot of problems." Her parents maintained an abusive relationship, both with one another and with her. At school, she was distracted by thoughts of her home situation and remembers spending a lot of time just staring out the classroom window daydreaming. As a result, learning to read was slow and difficult. To complicate matters, Maria had almost no opportunity to get the individual attention she needed from teachers. "When I told them I didn't know the words, they wouldn't sit down with me and help me. There were too many kids. That's what they always used to say."

When she was 10 years old, Maria was institutionalized for reasons she has never fully understood. This much she does know:

> I tried to ask for help, that my mother was beating me up a lot and they didn't want to hear me because they listened to my mother more than they listened to me. So, they figured that I'd try to run away from home and all this . . . that I had too many problems . . . so they put me away for five years of my life. When I came out I was under so much medication that my brain wasn't functioning right for awhile.

Once Maria returned to public school, she was a different kind of student than she had been before. "I didn't ask for too much help. . . . I just tried to do the best I could with my own time." In the evenings, in privacy, an older sister would help her with homework. When in class, she tried as best she could to commit lessons to memory.

Over time, Maria became more openly resistant to conventions of the classroom. For example, reading out loud was expected of all the students but Maria refused. She said, "I just didn't want to deal with the problem again. [The teacher] would fail me every time for not reading out loud." Often she would avoid going to class altogether.

Because Maria never was able to achieve a high enough reading level, she received a certificate rather than a diploma when she finished the twelfth grade. Shortly thereafter, she married Jesus, who had been her high school boyfriend, and they began a family.

Maria's life now centers around children—her own, her sister's, those she cares for at the child care center where she works, and those she teaches in a Sunday school Bible class. Maria's motivation as an adult to become a better reader and writer was partially rooted in the responsibility she feels toward the children in her life. When her daughter began having trouble keeping up in school, it became clear to Maria that she would have to improve her own abilities in order to help. "I was the one that had to help her," she explained, "because my husband works at night and there is nobody to sit down and help her."

Maria's desire to change was also fueled by feelings she had about herself. "I felt bad," she says, "I needed to do something for myself. And learn more. I don't like being like this." Maria recalls a series of incidents contributing to her poor self-image and her desire to change:

When Jesus was sick one time I had to fill out an application. I didn't even know how to read it and I had to tell the people, "I can't read, can you help me out?" And it made me feel like . . . nothing, you know? He really was sick for a long time and he didn't have a job so I had to go to Public Assistance and I had to fill out applications and I didn't even know how to read them. Everybody had to help me. I didn't go to work out in the city because I didn't know how to fill out applications. One time I went to the unemployment office to get a job and they told me, "Oh you have a high school diploma?" I said no. Then when they gave me an application to fill out, I couldn't even fill it out either. I had to ask somebody next to me.

Unlike Maria, Jesus has always been a competent reader who enjoys reading for both pleasure and purpose. In the past, he felt some tension and sadness around the fact that Maria was not able to share his love of the written word:

Reading is exciting and a lot of times I'll come across something that thrills me and I want to share it because sometimes it's better if that person can read that for themselves. There are some self-help books which maybe I think she could read like with . . . that may deal with the problem of children. It's not an easy thing to raise them and so I read this or some kind of exciting stories.

Jesus admits that Maria's reading difficulty was often a source of tension between them. He had a hard time understanding how someone could not read since reading came so easily for him. Jesus says, "Sometimes I used to blow my stack. . . . So then I thought about, well let's get you involved in a program." Maria considers Jesus' encouragement and practical assistance crucial to her actually making the move to join a literacy program. "You know, he had to be my phone caller and writing all the information down because I didn't know how to do all of that. He always wanted me to learn how to read, too. I think he was more the one who pushed me more into it, too."

Life Inside the Program: "We're Just Like a Family"

Maria says she's "picky" when it comes to choosing a literacy program. "I look for someone who's really going to help me," she says. One of the first programs she attended was sponsored by the library. Maria never liked the library program because

> the teacher didn't hardly talk. You didn't know too much about him. He didn't open up to you. He just sat there, he gave you the work, that's it. Like high school kids. You're on your own. And I didn't like that. He didn't know if you had any problems or anything. So he never even bothered asking you.

After the library program Maria tried a program offered through the public school system that focused exclusively on preparing students to pass the GED. She knew that she needed to improve her reading before she would be able to study independently using the GED workbooks like other students, but this kind of assistance was not available. Maria says that they would "tell you to read but they wouldn't be sitting down with you and helping you with reading." Maria was further frustrated by the fact that the teacher often failed to show up. It was not long before she quit attending the GED program.

Jesus encouraged Maria to try LVNYC after hearing about it on television. Now, Maria goes to LVNYC two evenings a week for about 3 hours. Here she feels satisfied with both the tutors and the instructional program. LVNYC's emphasis on improving reading and writing is just what Maria had hoped to find. She also likes the fact that much of the instruction occurs in small groups with students working together. She explains that

> over here, they sit down and they help you a lot. And everybody around you, you work together with everybody . . . it's not you by yourself. And I like it. If you have a problem, they'll help you here. . . . They really make you feel at home. They make you feel like you're a part of it.

Maria agrees with another student in her tutoring group who describes the way in which "by all of us putting a letter here and a letter there, you know we get it together. We're more of a family than just students."

Maria likes the fact that students choose the books they will read rather than having books chosen for them. And she appreciates the fact that she can bring materials in from "the outside world," like applications and other forms, and the tutors will help her with these. LVNYC offers driver's education and Bible study classes, which Maria pursues with great interest and enthusiasm. She adds, "I like it, you know what, because they don't treat you like little kids."

Maria learned writing strategies early in the program, such as writing the first letter followed by a line for words she does not know how to spell and then moving on until she can get help. She also found it helpful for group members to read together since someone always seems to know a word that others do not. When reading alone, she says the key is not to stop. She explains, "What I do is I get a little pad, write the words down but continue to read. The object is not to quit. When the book is too hard, I'll just get another one that's a little easier."

After experiencing some initial progress in the program, Maria began to involve Jesus and her children in reading and writing activities. In fact, home life and group life began to look very much alike when it came to learning. Maria's family members discuss books and videos as a way of spending time together. Likewise, in her tutoring group "everybody chips in" with writing projects by contributing topics. Maria organizes time at home so that everyone reads at the same time with the TV off for set periods. In the group it works the same way: "You know if everybody is reading you got to read . . . you can't be writing. That's no problem." The same excitement for learning in the group extends into the home and in both places learning occurs collaboratively. Maria's daughter describes what goes on at home now:

> She made a deal with me. She helped me with my social studies and I helped her with the driving test. I would ask her questions. Very good the first 20. And then she'd ask me questions, the first 20 questions. So we were both learning. And it worked so good because she likes math and I hate math. She hates social studies and I like social studies. . . . All of a sudden she would make it exciting and I wouldn't want to stop.

Maria describes similar excitement in the group when she says, "I really love the group. They're more alive. They're active. And it makes you feel like you . . . I don't know how . . . they make you feel comfortable, relaxed."

Maria is aware that particular learning strategies work better for her than others. She uses what she's learned in the tutoring group about effective instruction to help members of her family at home. For example, she'd like to help Jesus pass his driver's exam: "I told him I help him because the way my driver's ed. teacher taught me I might be able to help him visual instead. You see he may remember it better by visual than just reading." Similarly, Maria wants to see a friend in her tutoring group experience success, too, so she offers up suggestions to the tutor:

So I told [my tutor] why don't you bring in some tapes and let him read along with the book. Do flash cards. You know like give him easy words. You know and like that. She said that's a good idea. And when I saw this kid, he was reading a driver's ed. book. And I said I can't believe it! He was really improved. He came into the reading really good. And I hear him reading and he's writing and I felt so good. I said you know he can do it!

Just as Maria expects the members of her family to support one another in any circumstance, she wants her tutoring group to be supportive, stable, and predictable. About herself, she says, "I try not to do it . . . not to quit. Because I was a quitter a lot of times. . . . I'll do anything. I stay here til . . . I come in at 5. I stay until 8. And I leave at 8 when everybody leaves. . . . It takes a lot of hard work and study." She would like others to share her commitment. She says of the other group members: "I just hope they don't separate. You know, as far as breaking apart . . . leaving. . . . You feel a little uncomfortable when they go for a long time and then they come back. It changes but you always try to make them feel comfortable."

Maria says that she can become discouraged when others around her get discouraged. This awareness feeds her desire to keep the group as cohesive as possible.

It makes you more discouraged when they say they can't do it. Because you know they could. Because if you can do it and you've come from a person that didn't even know how to read the word "I" or "the" . . . if you can read now . . . I know somebody who didn't even know how to read the word.

Maria explains that she "builds herself up" by building up other people. But it works the other way, too. She says, for instance, "Sometimes I come in real down and depressed and they do it to me. . . . They all cheer you up a little bit back and forth."

Although Maria has not been tested yet, she says that she can now read books written on a fourth-grade level. Also, she describes feeling more confident lately and willing to "take more chances."

Life Outside the Program: "Going Toward That 'Why Not?'"

Since entering the program, Maria feels more competent with the reading and writing required of her at work. She is also more accepting of what she perceives as her limitations and less embarrassed about revealing them to others. Rather than avoiding certain situations, as she might have in the past, Maria now seeks out opportunities to learn alongside the children she cares for.

> [When] they were babies they didn't read so you just made up your own little story about the Bible. And then they would do arts and crafts. And that's it. Now it's a little heavier because now you have to read with them. But we all read as a group and when I make a mistake they help me, and when they make a mistake I help them. The kids know that I have trouble reading. So we all work together as one family.

Maria realizes, "[Now] like I wouldn't be embarrassed if somebody tells me go and spell this for the kids. And I would do it. . . . When I have trouble, I come to the [day care] teacher and he helps me out with some of the spellings and then I go help [the kids]." She is also discovering what accounts for normal reading behavior and sees herself more within that norm.

> Every time I read I always make sure there's not too many people around. I read pretty much out loud to myself. I see people coming in. Then I lower my voice a little. But I found out a lot of people do that. . . . I'm not crazy reading to myself.

Maria's family notices that she is changing, too. Jesus describes a major shift in Maria's perspective since she has been in the program:

> Before she'd use the past as an excuse. And like there was no way to change it. Like I think it was Robert Kennedy who said some people see things as they are and ask why and they get stuck in the why, you know. And so they never advance. And then some people dream things that never were and ask why not. And now she's going toward that why not. . . . Instead of getting stuck and not ever changing, she's going forward. She's motivated.

As Maria changes, her relationships with family members change, too. She finds the tension easing in her relationship with Jesus now that she asks him for help a lot less often. Likewise, the children say they are no longer awakened in the night to spell a word or distracted from their homework to help their mother read something. Everyone talks about how proud they are of Maria for her accomplishments.

There are still a few things Maria would like to do better. She has yet to become comfortable using the automatic teller machine at her bank, for instance. She says that she has trouble reading the directions as quickly as the computer demands and so she panics. Maria would also like to travel more on the subways. She recently rode alone on the subway for the first time and was able to read all the signs for all the stops. But there are some neighborhoods, like the Bronx, where she remains fearful of traveling. This, she says, is because "you can get lost a lot faster there since everything is reading . . . there's no numbers." Maria still wants to pursue her plans for the future, like getting a GED, going to college, or owning and operating her own day care center. She believes she will probably continue to experience success since, in her view, she is a determined person. And she says, "I don't quit easily." Jesus agrees and adds, "I've seen her be so motivated that I think that if she accelerates even more I think there'll be no stopping her."

6

The Program: Literacy Volunteers of New York City in 1990

Lawrence, Marsha, Don, Ann, and Maria experience and understand learning at Literacy Volunteers of New York City (LVNYC) differently. To place their stories in context, we offer this profile of the program itself at the time of the original study.

LVNYC has engaged in its own continuing evolution since 1990, with the volunteer program becoming part of a more extensive organization in the years since this study. In 1990, however, LVNYC provided small-group tutoring at 10 different sites (which they called centers) in Manhattan, Brooklyn, and the Bronx during the period of this study. The participants' enthusiasm transforms the sterile corporate office buildings into warm learning environments.

A large, modern corporate bank building in midtown Manhattan looms over the rush hour crowds filing into the subway entrance. A few adults go in the opposite direction, emerging from the subway to make their way past the guard station in the building to the elevator banks. As they emerge on the seventh floor and turn right toward the cafeteria, they see a handmade sign with an arrow and "Literacy" written in different colors pointing the way down the long hallway to the lunchroom.

The lunchroom itself is long and narrow; floor-to-ceiling partitions and columns divide up the length to give the appearance of a series of smaller rooms. The ceilings are low and the lights are recessed. All along the length of the cafeteria are floor-to-ceiling windows that look out on a terrace and, beyond that, at surrounding office buildings. On this early spring evening, the lights of the lunchroom reflect in the large windows. Inside, the carpets, chairs, and walls are a burnished red. Some tables are round and some are rectangular.

Three people from "Ben's group" are already seated at one of the long tables. Vito, Carla, and Teresa are talking together and occasionally laughing. Next to them is another long table covered with about 60 different books and papers on many different subjects. Teresa is originally from the Caribbean, and Carla is African-American. Both women are in their late twenties. Vito is an older Caucasian man. All have been attending LVNYC for at least a year. Ben, also Caucasian, is in his thirties and arrives a little after 5:00 P.M. Georgia, a middle-aged African-American woman, arrives a few minutes later.

Ben's group meets for two hours twice a week; as each person joins the group, everyone else greets the newcomer and asks how he or she is doing. On this particular evening, Ben reminds them they will be going to a taping of a popular situation comedy next week and tells them they can bring guests. Vito, who is married, teases the single Teresa that she might meet "Mr. Right" at the show. Ben tells her, "Don't let him get to you," with good humor.

At 5:12, Ben says, "Let's go over what everyone's reading this week." Carla is reading about Ray Charles and tells the group how he became blind around the age of 2, which surprises Georgia, who comments she thought he was blind from birth. Next Ben asks Georgia, "How's *Fatherhood?*" referring to the book by Bill Cosby. Georgia shrugs, saying she's not getting that much out of it. Ben replies he feels the same about a book someone recommended to him, *The Handmaid's Tale*. He is not sure what he thinks of the book. Meanwhile Georgia pulls out her book and pages through it until she finds a section that was funny to her. She recounts it to the group in her own words, occasionally using dialogue style to get her ideas across.

At another center, a different scene unfolds:

Students take the elevator to a large room on the 25th floor that is divided into large cubicles. The groups have a lot of space between them. Two African-American men are seated at four small tables pushed together to accommodate at least six more people. Billy is reading the *New York Post* and Alfred is writing words in his notebook as he reads a speech by Malcolm X from a pamphlet. A third, older African-American man, Oscar, joins the group, which has two young Caucasian women, Janice and Karen, as tutors. Don, another African-American man, is the last to arrive. Oscar engages Karen in a discussion about a visit by the program director. He is upset because he misunderstood the date of the visit. It is not tonight. Janice and Karen talk quietly to different students who are reading their books. Following silent reading and a brief question-and-answer period, the group begins writing.

There is a palpable shift in energy. Everyone seems more interested and alert. Janice moves around to sit next to Don to look at his writing. Oscar gives Alfred advice, telling him to write until he's happy with it or until he's finished. Then he can read it to the group or get it published. Alfred isn't too sure he's ready to go public, commenting, "I'm going to keep this literature in the family." Oscar volunteers that he wrote about homeless people.

Billy moves to sit next to Karen so he can read his writing and figure out where the punctuation goes. As he reads, he recognizes that "something's not right, here." Karen reads to him so he can hear it and talk with her about what he means to say. He works on the rewording and tells her to "put 'will' in." She tells him he can do it since it is his piece. She continues to read along and make suggestions to make it more clear.

Alfred asks how to spell "humid." Janice suggests Oscar reread his writing and think some more about what he wants to say. Oscar shows her his work, and she writes the symbol for the temperature in degrees (a small circle) for him.

Janice moves to assist Don, who wants help organizing all the ideas he has. With Janice asking questions, he talks about what he means. The group is lively and involved.

LVNYC is a complex program that included student leadership development, tutor training, and publishing as important components during the period of this study. For our purposes, this profile focuses on the instructional program; it should be remembered that it is set in an environment of complementary services and structures.

Instructional groups are the primary mechanism for student immersion in a literacy-rich environment. Each group we observed at LVNYC organized time differently, but there were some common patterns that reflect tutor training. All sessions tend to have some reading (silent or oral) followed by a short discussion, and some writing, also followed by discussion. Students often read to the group what they have written, and some tutors will take final versions of pieces home to type for students.

The relative amount of time spent on reading and writing varies from group to group and, sometimes, from session to session of the same group. Sometimes there is a schedule (e.g., Mondays have more reading and a little writing and Wednesdays have more writing and a little reading) but often the tutors seem to respond to the group's needs and interests. Some tutors plan sessions on specific skills, such as phonic analysis or using the dictionary, often following writing. Sometimes an entire session might be preempted to work on special topics such as job applications or voter registration.

Students read "real" books rather than workbooks to improve their reading at LVNYC. This allows students to work directly on the literacy practices they want to bring into their lives, rather than first studying in workbooks and then trying to "transfer" their reading skills to new practices.

LVNYC 's approach to reading instruction stresses meaning and context; the methods are chosen to encourage students to be more concerned with understanding the overall meaning of what they are reading than with being able to "call" individual words. When students read out loud, they sometimes substitute words with meanings similar to those in the text, and the tutors see this kind of attention to meaning as a "good" error.

Emphasizing meaning challenges programs like LVNYC to provide a wide range of reading materials with diverse content. Lawrence's comments were echoed by many other students: "More books, got to have more books. . . . They have a small selection, but you want more than that. Some of those selections are like the pits, and I mean, you know, you get bored."

The use of oral reading in addition to, or instead of, silent reading is controversial in the program. Students often enjoy oral reading; they assist each other and support each other's efforts. Students who want to retain oral reading in the program often know that they are proponents of a school model that comes from their earlier experiences. But they feel they learn best that way and want that knowledge respected by the program. They also enjoy the social interaction of oral reading. In addition, some students comment that oral reading allows them to make a connection between their internal "voice" and their "out loud voice," a profound insight for new readers.

We saw students writing in all of the centers at LVNYC—with their groups or sitting alone before or after class. Students proudly display their notebooks and folders filled with writing and enthusiastically share the stories behind their stories.

Some tutors use reading as a foundation for writing; students write about their books or about content related to their books. Usually, though, writing is a discrete activity and students are encouraged to write about whatever they are interested in. This results in a great deal of personal reflection as the topic for writing, but some students also write about current events or about their daily experiences. Approaches to writing were consistent across the groups we observed, and emphasized meaning and communication rather than technical skills, at first. The entire tutoring group—tutors and students—often helps individuals find topics to write about and many students use their immediate personal experience.

Students read their writing to each other at each meeting, and they respond to each other's ideas with interest and support. Students tend to cheer each other on while tutors spend time trying to fashion more substantive feedback. Tutors often help students through many revisions and then encourage students to submit their work for publication in one of the books or newsletters published by the program. Students usually keep their writing; they are proud of their work and share many drafts of their pieces with the interviewers. In addition, Literacy Volunteers of New York City maintains an extensive publishing program that is very important to students. Publishing provides a tangible incentive for writing and immediate feedback that is important for supporting changes in self-concept.

Students describe writing as a way to express their feelings and ideas, as a way to develop abilities that will help them outside the program, and, sometimes, as a political act. Two students spoke with us about writing letters to city officials about conditions they found intolerable; one woman spoke about writing a letter to protest how students had been treated at a national literacy conference. Writing is always a social act in these tutoring groups, while reading—especially when it is silent—feels far more solitary.

Control in the Instructional Program

Issues about control are central to learner-centered literacy work, and they have to be negotiated time and again (see Candy, 1991; Fingeret et al., 1994). LVNYC's belief in literacy as a process of constructing meaning is intended to respect students' experience and to honor the meanings they bring to their work in the program; students are viewed as having control over the content of what they read and write and over the focus of instruction. Tutors and staff try to develop an environment at LVNYC in which there is a predictable sequence of activities and in which students feel that they have some control over the environment and their own learning.

At the same time, however, LVNYC tutors and staff appear to feel responsible for helping students to "solve" their problems, retaining control in many situations. Tutors do not seem aware of a problem-posing stance in which they could work together with students to place an issue in some larger perspective. In addition, the fundamental issues of instructional approach are decided as program policies, rather than being open to negotiation between tutors and students. Thus, tensions develop in the program around issues of authority and control.

"There For You": Tutors

Students who like their tutors usually describe a combination of personality characteristics and good teaching skills; not only do they like the tutor, they also believe they are learning. Students appreciate having tutors' telephone numbers. They call if they are unable to come to class, and students feel that their tutors are available for assistance with homework or literacy practices. When tutors are "there" for students, this includes helping with a wide range of problems. For example, Lawrence says that if he has problems at home, he can talk to his tutor "on the side."

Students who have been in the program for any substantial period of time have had to deal with losing tutors with whom they have established trust, and "breaking in" new tutors who are often fresh out of training. Students often have developed means of coping with these changes, and they share their strategies with each other. The students' descriptions of what happens when they lose effective tutors is consistent across all of the students who participated with us. It is a picture of moving forward and then treading water, followed by some (small or large) regression, followed by new learning, in positive cases, or frustration in other cases. Students clearly feel there is a "cost" when effective tutors leave; it varies only in degree.

Sometimes students are uncomfortable with what feels like an unequal relationship. Most of the tutors are white and middle class, quite different from the students; we did not observe classroom conversation that appeared to be raising issues specifically concerning the students' ethnic, racial, linguistic, or class backgrounds. Thus, students are left on their own to figure out how their participation in LVNYC can have an impact on their engagement in the world outside of the classroom, to the extent that their situations are shaped by social, political, and cultural forces as well as by their literacy abilities.

Conclusion

LVNYC provides a structure within which there is great flexibility as the program attempts to meet the needs of students such as Lawrence, Marsha, Don, Ann, and Maria. The program's emphasis on writing helps students become more reflective and feel more assertive. The use of group instruction enables the development of a sense of community and family, in some cases. Tutors' attention to individuals allows students to progress at their own pace while supporting each other. However, there are still limits to LVNYC's effectiveness and its ability to respond to students' characteristics and situations. Some students are frustrated by group instruction, tutor turnover, daily writing assignments, and instructional policy mandates, for example.

Lawrence, Marsha, Don, Ann, and Maria experience a "fit" between their characteristics and LVNYC to differing degrees. This helps us understand some of the differences in the extent to which these learners change their lives. While effective instruction is crucial to change, however, it fits within a much larger framework of factors and conditions that enable or inhibit movement.

SECTION II

A Framework for Change

In this section we propose a framework for how adults move through a profound transformation of identity and world-view as they move further into the literate culture. We propose that culture and literacy practices are interwoven; it is not possible to change one without an impact on the other. We draw heavily on a model proposed by Lofland and Stark (1965) for identity change; they applied the model to religious conversion, but were primarily concerned with the deeper process of identity transformation in a multitude of contexts. Our framework is based on the profiles included in Section I, the larger data base of this study (Fingeret & Danin, 1991), and the existing research literature in adult literacy.

7

Contexts for Literacy

Lawrence, Marsha, Don, Ann, and Maria illustrate change in differing degrees. They are all in a literacy program, but their stories tell of changes that are broader than improved performance in school. We need a way of understanding literacy and change that incorporates all the myriad forms it takes. For this purpose we draw upon Lytle and Wolfe's (1989) explanation of literacy as skills, tasks, practices, and critical reflection and action. Then, focusing on literacy as social and cultural practices, we propose a framework for change.

Literacy Contexts and Purposes

The prevailing notion of literacy among educators and the general public focuses on reading, and emphasizes discrete *technical skills* that can be applied across contexts and cultures. The so-called independent reader is provisioned with a toolbox of skills such as phonics analysis, syllabication, and main idea identification. With such tools the reader is supposed to be able to deal with any literacy situation that arises. This kind of "autonomous model" of literacy, according to Street (1992), assumes that literacy exists separately from specific situations or ideologies. In this model, meaning resides in the text itself; consequently, many literacy educators focus on decoding and encoding as instructional goals. Instruction focuses on words, and then on how words build sentences and paragraphs.

A slightly more complex conception of literacy views literacy as the ability to independently and successfully accomplish specific *tasks* such as filling in forms, pulling information from newspaper ads, or addressing an envelope. There is some sense of context here, since these tasks are socially constructed (that is, they have been created by our society, rather than existing in nature), but there remains the assumption that successful accomplishment of these tasks is stable across situations and requires only applying individual technical skill achievement. In other words, instructors consider filling in a form in an employment office to be the same task as filling in that form while sitting in literacy class.

Both of these conceptions of literacy fall short of incorporating a more complex understanding of independence or, actually, an understanding of interdependence as the underlying nature of social life. Viewing literacy as skills or literacy as tasks separates adults from their knowledge about the world and defines literacy as a process of getting the meaning from the texts rather than as constructing meaning through interaction with texts and the social world.

Educators who subscribe to Street's (1992) autonomous view of literacy reinforce the illusion that independence occurs in the abstract, rather than being tied to specific times, places, and persons. This is despite the fact that most adults have experienced a sudden loss of their sense of independence when confronted with a new environment, a new task, or a new situation. Our folklore is full of stories of city people moving to the country and vice versa; the empathy and amusement these tales engender, reflect our response to the plight of people who are applying social norms inappropriately across situations.

Viewing literacy as skills or tasks does not adequately encompass the complexity of the experience of literacy in adults' daily lives. Literacy reflects the fundamental interdependence of the social world at many levels; oral language is a shared understanding of a set of relationships between symbols, sounds, and meanings. Meaning reflects shared cultural heritage, individual personality, and unique life experiences. Although literacy requires knowledge of the technical skills of forming letters, spelling words, decoding, and so on, these technical skills are useless without social knowledge that attaches meaning to words *in context*. For example, a letter from the Department of Social Services describing its services has different meanings to a potential welfare recipient than it does to a tenured university professor studying the welfare system. Literacy as skills denies the role of meaning in literacy; literacy as tasks denies the role of social context.

Adults engage in social and cultural literacy *practices;* they do not create literacy brand new each time, but rather interact with the shared meanings and functions of literacy in their environments. We now have a number of studies that show how literacy practices differ across cultures, partly because the meanings connected to language and action differ in these cultural settings (e.g., Heath, 1980, 1983; Reder & Green, 1985; Scribner & Cole, 1981). This view of literacy moves beyond skills and tasks to recognize the role of meaning and context explicitly. Literacy cannot be separated from the system of ideas in a specific setting, and adults use literacy within their social and cultural contexts to manipulate the system, trying to get their needs met.

Literacy practices often occur in contexts that value independent action and obscure the social nature of literacy. When adults aspire to new literacy practices, they also are aspiring to the images of literate adults that are promoted in the larger society, and to the society's values of independent action. Literacy practices, because they are situated, imply not just doing tasks, but doing them *as other people do them in the same situation*. The new literacy practices they envision are not discrete goals; they are examples of ways that adult learners would like to "fit in," to do things the way others do them without drawing attention to themselves and without feeling uncomfortable. Even when adults talk about their goals in terms of social and economic mobility, they are aspiring to *act* like people act at other rungs of the social ladder. This includes, but is by no means limited to, technical reading and writing abilities.

The view of literacy as practices recognizes that meanings change as situations change; however, it accepts the meanings in situations as nonproblematic. A fourth conception of literacy, as *critical reflection and action*, problematizes those meanings; it makes the context an explicit subject of analysis and reflection and proposes that it is possible to act to change the situation itself. For example, literacy educators may help learners develop their ability to use checking accounts at their local bank— learners engage in new practices. Educators engaged in critical reflection and action may help learners question the relationship between the bank, the local economy, community development, and the global marketplace. The work of critical theorists such as Paulo Freire and Henry Giroux is associated with this view of literacy. When adults have a critical perspective on the political and social nature of literacy, they can engage in action that uses literacy as a tool in an intentional way.

The adults who participated in this study do not want to keep the line waiting at the bank or the grocery store; they do not want to draw attention to themselves on the subway platform as they struggle to figure out which side will have the uptown train. But appropriate behavior in specific situations varies from culture to culture. Shopping at the neighborhood store where everyone knows everyone else requires different interpersonal etiquette than does shopping at a large impersonal supermarket. Driving in a big city differs from driving in a small town. Students are developing a repertoire of socially situated and culturally appropriate literacy practices. Ferdman (1990) explains that as individuals move among situations, "in a culturally heterogeneous society, literacy ceases to be a characteristic inherent solely in the individual. It becomes an interactive process that is constantly redefined and renegotiated, as the individual transacts with the socioculturally fluid surroundings" (p. 187).

Adults cannot learn literacy practices in the abstract; they are learning about becoming literate persons in specific social and cultural contexts (see, for example, Center for Literacy Studies, 1992; Ferdman, 1990; Freire, 1985; Horsman, 1991; Hunter, 1990; Klassen, 1991; Parker, 1991; Weinstein-Shr, 1990). Independent social action means that adults are acting in relation to a situation, taking into account other people, social and cultural norms, their own experience, and, of course, the technical knowledge they need to encode or decode (Ferdman, 1990). Therefore, when we talk of change and literacy in the framework that follows, we are referring to changes in literacy practices, reflecting the socially situated nature of literacy.

Viewing literacy as practices recognizes some of the political and cultural dimensions of literacy; Street (1992) calls this an "ideological" model of literacy. The ideological model respects the social nature of literacy, and the political nature of action. Literacy has always been connected to power; even in ancient times literacy was connected to controlling information and resources. In modern times we've used literacy as a weapon to disenfranchise people and to maintain subjugation and slavery. Literacy is used as an indicator of full status as a member of the human race. It is used as an indicator of class and cultural status.

Literacy—even when viewed as practices—is not an end in itself. It is always connected to some broader purpose, as described by Stein (1995) through her analysis of literacy students' writing about literacy. Stein explains:

> When we talk about "purposes" here, however, we are not talking about these context- or time-specific accomplishments, but about more fundamental purposes that express the social and cultural meaning or significance of these accomplishments for individuals engaged in defining themselves as competent actors in the world. (p. 9)

The larger purposes that surface in her analysis are:

> Literacy for Access and Orientation
> Literacy as Voice
> Literacy for Independent Action
> Literacy as a Bridge to the Future (p. 10)

Furthermore, she continues:

> Adult students don't make [a] separation between literacy for life and literacy for the workplace or for citizenship. While the specific tasks, roles and

responsibilities vary from context to context, the four fundamental purposes remain the same. Moreover, these purposes of education—what adults need literacy for—drive the acquisition of skills and knowledge both within and across contexts. Adults seek to develop literacy skills in order to change what they can do, how they are perceived and how they perceive themselves in specific social and cultural contexts. (p. 10)

Lawrence, Marsha, Don, Ann, and Maria help us understand the process through which adult literacy students change their literacy practices and, as they move through this process, change their images of themselves and, therefore, change their lives.

A Framework for Change

Each of the adults in our profiles engages in a unique process of change; nonetheless, there are patterns underlying their movement. We propose a framework for how adults transform their identity as they move into literate culture that is adapted from Lofland and Stark (1965). The framework posits literacy as cultural and social practices, and it helps us understand the role of personal agency. We recognize that, for those adults who manage to experience deep and profound change in their identity as literate people, their own personal resources, perspective, and hard work play a central role. However, this is not a deficit perspective. It places personal agency in relation to other conditions that are important to the change process, such as the social, political, and economic environment; effective instruction; and community. It also allows us to place previous conversations about literacy development in a broader framework (see Figure 7.1).

The overall image is one of a spiral (see Figure 7.2), since change is an iterative and dynamic process that occurs at varying rates (Lofland & Lofland, 1995). We are concerned with one turning of the spiral, as it moves through five stages: prolonged tension; turning point; problem solving and seeking educational opportunities; changing relationships and changing practices; and intensive continuing interaction. The first two can be considered background conditions because, for the most part, they take place outside the educational context. The last three are more situational, emphasizing the interaction between the educational situation and an adult's personal situation and illuminating the social nature of learning and change. For some adults, the spiral is longer, with many turnings, as change is pursued across a variety of contexts, over a long period of time. For others, the spiral is shorter, as adults exit from the process to pursue other avenues in their lives.

Figure 7.1: The Framework and Its Relationship to Adult Education Literature

Type of Condition	Stage in Framework	Concepts in the Literature
Background	Prolonged Tension	Prior schooling experience Self-esteem and self-concept Literacy as practices Autonomous vs. ideological literacy Shame
Background	Turning Point	Social network theory Adult development theory Perspective transformation Participation theory
Situational	Problem Solving and Seeking Educational Opportunities	Prior adult education experiences Inside and outside domains Public and private practices Intentional change
Situational	Changing Relationships and Changing Practices	Pushing and crossing boundaries Social network theory Literacy program impact studies
Situational	Intensive Continuing Interaction	Adult development theory Social learning theory

This framework is our first attempt at depicting the process through which change appears to occur for many adults who participate in literacy programs with the larger goal of changing their lives. It is not intended to provide a blueprint for change, nor is it expected to portray the process for every adult. It is offered here as a step in the continuing theoretical discussion of literacy education and change. It builds on previous depictions of literacy program impact that focused almost exclusively on frequency of outcomes (e.g., Darkenwald & Valentine, 1984), without attempting explanation. All of those familiar outcomes such as improvement in self-esteem and increased independence with literacy practices can be found within this framework. We have placed them in a broader framework, however, to try to show how those outcomes are part of a larger process of change in which adults are engaging. We also try to show how impacts that are usually portrayed as discrete are related to each other.

Figure 7.2   The Spiral of Change

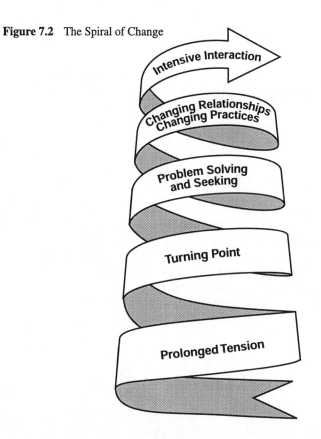

This framework requires that we think of learning and personal change as inextricably bound up together. It requires that we think deeply about the social nature of learning, change, and literacy. Although the adult learners in our profiles generously volunteered to help us learn about these issues, we can find evidence of this process by simply turning inward and examining our own lives.

8

Background Conditions

The first two factors in the framework predispose adults to change (Lofland & Stark, 1965); we present these as background conditions. The first, prolonged tension, may exist for a long time before it contributes to action and change. Many factors contribute to tension building, including social, emotional, cultural, economic, and historical circumstances. However, at some point circumstances change and new possibilities emerge for many adults. They channel their resources in response to this turning point, the second background condition, seizing it as an opportunity for initiating larger changes in their lives.

Prolonged Tension

Many people feel a discrepancy between the way life is and the way they think it could be. This is at the heart of the background condition described by Lofland and Stark (1965) as *prolonged tension*. For the adults in our profiles, this sense of discrepancy is particularly acute. Shame often holds them back from resolving this tension.

Many adults with limited abilities to engage in literacy practices feel ashamed of their literacy problems. This often is learned very young, as children are left back in primary school or are taunted by their peers; Maria and Don describe traumatic early schooling experiences with repercussions that extend into adulthood. Most adults "learn" as children that their problems are their "fault"; they are told that they are stupid or aren't trying hard enough, or given other explanations that focus on their abilities. They never develop a critical analysis of their social world in which poor schooling, poverty, discrimination, crime, family situations, or other social and structural conditions share responsibility for slow progress in learning. Furthermore, the mass media contribute to self-blame and shame by laying the blame for economic problems on workers who have problems with literacy practices, reinforcing workers' self-blame rather than helping them to see themselves as caught in a web that includes social and political conditions beyond their control.

Some adults experience passing embarrassment when they are unable to participate in a literacy practice that others expect of them. Others go to great lengths to ensure that they do not find themselves in situations in which their inability to engage in literacy practices becomes publicly known. Many adults fall in between these two positions. They experience deep shame associated with their literacy abilities, and while it does not define their lives and their identities, it remains a force to be dealt with. Adults participating in this study discussed shame in a variety of ways. The roots of Don's deep shame about his literacy problems run all the way back to childhood memories of difficult schooling, family, and community experiences. Shame plays different roles for Lawrence, Marsha, Don, Ann, and Maria, a role that both affects and is affected by relationships with others in their lives.

Many adults in literacy programs do not feel comfortable with their own family members' knowing about their problems with literacy practices. Don, for example, identifies some of his siblings' attitudes as contributing to his shame. He has not felt comfortable practicing his writing at home or asking for help. Don has not let his friends know about his literacy problems; he says that this is to protect *them* from worrying about how to treat him. Maria's family, on the other hand, is characterized by trust and caring. Her relationship to shame is different, and the resources she calls on to support her learning are much broader and deeper. Ann's family knows that she is in a program, but she feels ashamed to ask them for help with her writing; she waits until she gets to class to ask for help.

Shame is a complex topic; a full exploration of shame is not possible here (see Bradshaw, 1988; Goldberg, 1991; and Kaufman, 1985 for extensive discussions of shame). However, there are some basic concepts about shame that can help us understand its role in creating prolonged tension and its power to obstruct change for Don and for other adult literacy students.

All of us experience shame in our lives; it has a useful and important function:

> Shame is the emotion which gives us permission to be human. Shame tells us of our limits. Shame keeps us in our human boundaries, letting us know we can and will make mistakes, and that we need help. . . . Healthy shame is the psychological foundation of humility. It is the source of spirituality. (Bradshaw, 1988, p. vii)

Shame often is a somewhat fleeting emotion, a response to a situation that we feel, note, deal with, and then move on.

Sometimes, however, shame is experienced repeatedly in early relationships with family members, peer groups, teachers, or members of a community. Don, for instance, describes feeling betrayed and publicly humiliated by his teachers. When this happens repeatedly, the bridge of trust is broken, and healthy shame, which has been connected to external sources, can be internalized in a toxic way. Shame becomes part of a person's identity and an external incident is no longer necessary for someone to feel shame (Kaufman, 1985). "For some people, being ashamed is only an occasional incident in their lives. For still others it is a continual sense of their being in the world" (Goldberg, 1991, p. 5).

Personal identity is constructed out of a complex network of social interactions. It includes self-concept, or one's overall set of beliefs and images about oneself (Sanford & Donovan, 1984; cited in Foster, 1989). It also includes self-esteem, which has to do with the value placed on those images as a result of comparison with some set of idealized images. Self-esteem can be negative in relation to some images and positive in relation to others, contributing to an overall negative or positive judgment about oneself. In this way we can understand that some adults think of themselves as quite competent in some areas while having low self-esteem in relation to schooling or literacy (Foster, 1989). Self-concept and self-esteem are socially developed; that is, they are developed as a result of the relationship between an individual and the social world.

Socially constructed shame can become internalized until it becomes part of one's vision of self. When shame becomes internalized, negative self-esteem is generalized beyond its connection to specific images, such as literacy abilities. The result is a painful way of being in the world.

> Our identity is that vital sense of who we are as individuals, embracing our worth, our adequacy, and our very dignity as human beings. All these can be obliterated through protracted shame, leaving us feeling naked, defeated as a person and intolerably alone. . . . Contained in the experience of shame is the piercing awareness of ourselves as fundamentally deficient in some vital way as a human being. To live with shame is to experience the very essence or heart of the self as wanting. (Kaufman, 1985, pp. 7–8)

Kaufman describes two types of defenses. One is aimed at protecting oneself against additional exposure and experiences of shame. Strategies for defense, such as rage, contempt, striving for power or perfection, or internal withdrawal are directed outward initially, toward external sources of shame. For example, Don's response to possible exposure and shame was developed in his childhood; he deals with his sense of powerlessness by acting angry and getting attention to his anger, or by withdrawing from social interaction. Many adults try to avoid situations that require engaging in literacy practices; this may include quitting or turning down jobs or promotions, as Ann did. Adults may also limit travel and activities to a narrow geographic area and refuse to develop intimate relationships for fear of discovery, like Don. Some adults also engage in behaviors that give the appearance of literacy, such as carrying newspapers or books or looking at bulletin boards on which notices are posted.

However, Kaufman (1985) explains, "certain defenses may later become directed inward and aimed at the very self of the defending individual. For instance, rage, contempt, and blame can be so turned against the self" (pp. 86–87). Self-blame can be reinforced through negative inner voices that reflect past experiences. Firestone (1988; cited in Goldberg, 1991) describes the contemptuous negative inner voices that continue scripts that were often first developed in childhood, supporting an individual's sense of self-blame and despair.

If we find ourselves already in a situation in which shame is beginning to be experienced, the second strategy seeks to transfer the feeling, decreasing one's own sense of shame by making someone else feel shame. For example, Don describes how he uses anger to turn attention away from his literacy abilities.

Literacy problems often are framed as problems of dependence today. A "lack" of independence has assumed shameful proportions:

> A . . . cultural injunction is to be independent and self-sufficient. Deeply imbedded in our cultural consciousness are images of the pioneer, cowboy, and more recently, the detective. These archetypal figures mirror how to stand proudly alone, never needing anything, never depending on anyone. Needing becomes not a source of strength, but a clear sign of inadequacy. To need is to be inadequate, shameful. . . . We are shamed for being human. (Pratt, 1990, p. 29)

The adults in our profiles often describe shame, embarrassment, and self-consciousness relating to literacy as pervasive in their lives. At the same time, they often experience themselves as competent workers, parents, citizens, and friends. This dissonance creates an internal tension for many adults who engage in limited literacy practices. This tension often is unwittingly exacerbated by educators and by the general public, which remain immersed in a skills-based or task-based conception of literacy.

Adults who engage in limited literacy practices often experience the world in a collaborative, interdependent manner that is at odds with the prevailing notions of independence. Their primary cultural orientation is often viewed negatively, judged within the normative framework of the dominant group's cultural patterns. However, research such as that of Fingeret (1982, 1983), Heath (1983), Reder (1987), and Reder and Green

(1985) provides insights into the culture of many adults who do not engage in extensive literacy practices.

For example, Fingeret (1982, 1983) conducted a field study with adults who participate in very limited literacy practices in their communities. In her conclusions, she proposes that we think of these adults primarily as members of oral subcultures, rather than as nonfunctioning members of the literate culture. Talk is at the heart of the oral subculture, and this requires consistent interaction, contradicting the prevailing assumption that nonreading adults are necessarily socially isolated, alienated, and inarticulate.

Adults with literacy problems find assistance with reading and writing practices from members of their communities and, in turn, they offer help with other tasks or information. For example, adults may provide child care assistance, insight into the politics of the welfare system, or knowledge about how to fix a car in exchange for help reading a letter or filling in a form.

Reder (1987) describes different types of knowledge that community members bring to a literacy task. These include "technological knowledge" or actual technical skills with reading and writing. Other members bring "functional knowledge," or an understanding of the relationship between the message and the way it is presented (i.e., in a form letter, a business letter, etc.) and "social knowledge," or an understanding of the meaning the literacy task has in a specific situation.

When this exchange process is viewed as mutually beneficial, adults see themselves as contributing members of their communities, and their limited literacy practices do not necessarily undermine a sense of independence. However, in the larger literate society the inability to read and write fluently defines inequality and incompetence, and interactions with the institutions (including media) of the larger society often result in adults with minimal literacy abilities feeling hindered and stigmatized by the limits of their literacy practices.

Viewing literacy as practices values adults' social and cultural knowledge, and, therefore, helps us understand students' tensions. For example, Lawrence may have trouble reading some of the safety rules at his job, but he understands the context within which the rules are to be applied. His knowledge of context *as well as* knowledge of decoding is necessary to understand the safety rules. Therefore, he experiences himself as knowledgeable but at the same time as limited. Of course, we all experience these tensions all the time; however, adults who can engage in limited literacy practices must also deal with a pervasive sense of shame and stigma attached to their limitations.

The quest for independent literacy practices is a quest to fit in, to do things the way the dominant culture does them, to remove a stigma and to become free of a deep source of shame by changing performance in particular circumstances. Adults who feel powerful in other areas of their lives seek a resolution to the tension introduced by their limited literacy practices. Maria echoes many adults when she says, "I don't like being like this."

Turning Points

Many adults who experience problems with literacy practices remain in that stressful situation for many, many years. As Lofland and Stark (1965) explain,

> First, people can persist in stressful situations with little or no relief. Second, persons often take specifically problem-directed action to change troublesome portions of their lives, without adopting a different world view to interpret them. . . . Third, a number of maneuvers exist to "put the problem out of mind." In general these are compensations for or distractions from problems in living. (p. 868)

In some cases, however, something happens to disrupt their coping patterns and new possibilities open. This *turning point,* according to Lofland and Stark (1965), is

> a moment when old lines of action were complete, had failed or been disrupted, or were about to be so, and when they faced the opportunity (or necessity), and possibly the burden, of doing something different with their lives. (p. 870)

This can take many forms: A child leaves home, a marriage dissolves, a worker is fired or takes a new job, a spouse or parent dies, a baby is born. The bonds of mutual obligation and expectation are weakened, making change feel more possible and, often, necessary and desirable (Fingeret, 1982). These times often feel like crises and problems; indeed, we see that Maria's husband became ill, providing the opportunity for change at the same time as increasing the need for change.

Some kind of event appears to be necessary for almost everyone in order to loosen the ties of obligation and tradition: Ann retired from her job; Lawrence and his girlfriend broke up; and Ann had the chance for a promotion on her job. Sometimes adults feel some control over the change, such as a choice to marry, divorce, or have a child. Many times, however, adults feel no control over changes in jobs or family situations, and struggle to find some way to be proactive in a situation not of their choosing. The challenge of the turning point often is to turn a perceived disaster into an opportunity.

These major turning points are the "trigger events" referred to by Aslanian and Brickell (1980). They have a "precipitating rather than a causative effect" (p. 27), releasing "a latent stream of activity driven by forces that have already built up a potential for action" (p. 27). Indeed, we see that students' decisions to enter a literacy program are usually part of a larger process of change in their lives that often involves changing relationships to family, friends, work, and themselves. For example, Lawrence felt better able to make a deeper commitment to his own growth and development after breaking up with his girlfriend, even though the breakup was painful for him at the time. He has gone on to lose weight, plan a vacation, see a counselor, and attend LVNYC.

We can view adults in literacy programs as being in the process of making a major life transition from more oral to more literate cultural participation and identity. Since these adults have been experiencing tension around literacy for many years, in most cases, we can look to the triggering event, or the major turning point, for insight into why the transition is occurring *now*. There will be many additional turning points along the way in the transition, as adults constantly assess their experience and decide what to do. These may be viewed as secondary turning points in relation to the initial trigger event.

Transitions are psychologically complex. For example, as Marsha develops her literacy practices, she is coping with the possibility of new job responsibilities, a new self-concept, new relationships with her family, and her aspirations for a new sociocultural position. While some of life's transitions are predictable, and related to adult development (see Merriam & Caffarella, 1991), many of the transitions in which the adults in this study are engaged were thrust upon them; they are dealing with an additional factor of coming to terms with a change they might not have chosen.

Adults deal with trigger events, or major turning points, in differing ways. In the cases of the adults here, relationships were central to the way they translated the trigger event into action. Felicia pushed Ann to attend LVNYC; Marsha and her mother came together; Don's mother showed him how to travel on the subway; and Maria's ill husband encouraged her in many ways. The form of support and the problems that were encountered differ widely, but it is clear that the turning point has to do with adults as socially situated actors in their lives, seeking assistance with change that will have an impact on the lives of many other people as well.

9

Situational Conditions
and Movement

Tension and turning points take place outside the educational context; they are rooted in adults' life circumstances and personal characteristics. Once an adult begins to consider new alternatives to resolving the tensions, however, educational programs play a role in the process. Adults seek out educational responses to their tensions and, as they engage in effective instruction, they begin to change their relationships and their practices. The change process is supported by intensive, continuing interaction with others inside and outside the program. The process then becomes iterative as new tensions arise and new opportunities are considered.

Problem Solving and Seeking Educational Opportunities

A major turning point creates stress and a time of reflection or *problem solving* (Lofland & Stark, 1965). Some adults will deal with their transition by using resources other than educational programs; others, however, will turn to educators for assistance in relieving the tension they experience. In some cases, this will be prior to a planned life transition, such as Marsha's preparation for a job change. Her development of new literacy practices, however, precipitates her life transition because of changes in other areas of her life, even though her job may not have changed yet. At other times, participation in education may be in the midst of a life transition, such as Maria's coping with her husband's illness.

Sometimes adults come to literacy programs asking for help with specific, discrete practices such as preparing for a driver's license test; they are worried about disrupting their social networks, for example, and want to relieve some of the tension they experience while minimizing larger change. In the terms we have been using here, they want to avoid a life transition but change literacy practices. Of course, being able to drive is itself a life transition and a change in identity. Putting boundaries and limits

on the extent of change is a struggle for learners that is often misunderstood by literacy practitioners (see Fingeret, 1982). Such limits can be
viewed as a lack of self-confidence or low aspirations rather than as an
attempt to control change and maintain existing social networks and
relationships. Seeking educational opportunities can lead to the creation
of other tensions and turning points. Adult learners may view these as
"costs" associated with their changes.

Seeking is not necessarily a well-organized quest driven by some
predesignated set of criteria. Often it is characterized by

> seemingly passive and chance strategies of *creative bumbling:* the individual
> seizes on potential opportunities for discovering a way of transforming his
> life within his sociocultural and circumstantial environment. As he acts, his
> self-conception as a "seeker" develops and he builds up an array of seeking
> tactics. Upon locating a promising means of life-change, he proceeds *creatively
> to exploit* its potentials by developing a further array of tactics . . . conceived
> here as intentional, utilitarian moves toward his goal of changing himself
> and his life. (Strauss, 1976, p. 253; emphasis in original)

For example, many of the adults in our profiles engaged in problem
solving and seeking by exploring other literacy programs before coming
to LVNYC. Although there is an emotional cost to program-hunting, it also
serves as a testing ground in which adults discover some things about themselves as learners. In places such as New York City, where there is a range
of possible programs, adults can learn to place themselves in relation to
those alternatives, choosing a program that appears to best meet their own
conception of their needs and strengths. Students can assess their experience in public school and previous adult literacy programs to create a
framework within which they evaluate their current program and teacher,
and they leave programs that do not suit them. For example, Lawrence
sees himself as a consumer investigating the extent to which a program
meets his needs; he has already left a program that felt inappropriate and
unresponsive.

Many adults in the United States do not have choices among programs;
sometimes they are lucky to have one program within reach. Their seeking and problem solving has to focus within that program as they search
for compatible teachers, tutors, schedules, fellow students, and learning
situations. The adults in our profiles often talk about the problems they
had at first with LVNYC's approach to instruction. Ann, for example,
wanted her tutor to tell her how to spell specific words rather than writing a line and moving on; others wanted to focus on phonics rather than
context or wanted to use workbooks. Some, like Maria and Lawrence, liked
group instruction while others disliked it intensely. Everyone who per-

sisted, however, was willing to try new ways of learning, and they judged the effectiveness of instruction in terms of changes in their lives, in their daily literacy practices. In addition, the program encouraged tutors to engage students in conversations about instruction, and to work with students to create instruction that was responsive and meaningful for learners. These conversations helped students understand the culture and language of the program better, which helped them communicate more effectively about their preferences.

As adults become involved in literacy programs during problem solving and seeking, their social world becomes divided into two domains, each with specific characteristics: *inside* and *outside* the program. Students often feel stigmatized by their problems with literacy outside the program. They know that they are viewed negatively by the larger social world, and often feel scared, isolated, exposed, or devalued when literacy is used in a situation. There often is less predictability outside the program, and higher levels of stress and anxiety. Students often feel the societal pressures for independent action and individual achievement keenly, and they suffer emotionally over their inability to meet those perceived demands. Students create social structures outside the program to provide some measure of security. Sometimes students are loners, trusting no one with knowledge about their literacy problems; other students involve trusted family members and friends in elaborate exchange networks.

Students know that information about their literacy abilities is known inside the program and that many other adults in the program have similar abilities and problems. Many students are seeking a program in which they feel valued rather than devalued, central rather than marginalized, part of a team rather than isolated. Students also want to feel that there is some amount of predictability inside the program.

LVNYC attempts to create a sense of program as community. As a result, there are many situations inside the program that provide opportunities for students to experience literacy as a social process. They interact with their small-group members, with their tutors, with others at their centers, with students from other centers at large program gatherings; if they want to, they can represent students in an advisory group or on the board of the organization. Students have many opportunities to engage in new literacy practices that involve other people and still are inside the program.

Situations inside and outside programs fall into two broad categories: private and public. Private and public situations have to do with the extent to which students *feel* private or public—that is, the extent to which they feel that they are controlling the information being communicated about them to others as well as the identities of those other persons. Situations feel more *private* when a student is alone or with well-known and trusted others, such as in their classes or with their families at home. However, when there are persons in the home with whom adults are not comfortable revealing their literacy problems, then home essentially becomes a public situation and the stress increases.

Situations feel more *public* when other people are involved who are not known and trusted, or when literacy use is open to the scrutiny of such persons. Students feel that they are in public situations inside the program when they help with teacher training, for example; outside the program, filling in a job application at a personnel office is a public situation. Situations feel more private when they feel contained and predictable; public situations lack limits and adults feel more exposed.

Most adults coming to literacy programs are used to revealing their literacy abilities only in private situations. In many instances only close family members know about an individual's struggles with literacy. Coming into a literacy program requires that adults become more public, sharing information with new people who may include program secretaries, intake counselors, teachers, tutors, fellow students, and testing administrators, as well as people involved in transportation to and from the site and people who are at the site for other reasons. Many students experience this as a process of moving from the private situation at home to a more public situation inside the program; they talk about building up nerve and courage to come. As students develop trust in their tutors or teachers and fellow students, classes take on many of the characteristics of private situations and students attempt to move out into public again, developing new literacy practices in their lives. If the group does not jell and trusting interpersonal relationships fail to become established, students continue to protect themselves, and the situation feels public even though it is inside the program. Students may leave, continuing to seek a program that feels comfortable and effective, or they may turn their attention elsewhere to resolve the tensions they experience around literacy.

Changing Relationships and Changing Practices

As learners explore educational opportunities and new possibilities for change emerge, *relationships* assume enhanced importance. Positive, accepting relationships with others inside the literacy program, including tutors, administrators, and fellow students, can mediate the sense of shame and isolation and support the development of enhanced self-esteem. Ann and Maria, for example, describe the centrality of their tutoring groups' sense of community. Changes in these relationships have an impact on learning as well; for example, Marsha and Don describe a deep sense of loss when their tutors left, and feel that their progress decreased for a time.

At the same time, relationships with others outside the program begin to change. Some students are relatively socially isolated and don't feel this as a pressure. For others, however, Lofland and Stark (1965) explain,

> when there were emotional attachments to outsiders who were physically present and cognizant of the incipient transformation, conversion became a "nip-and-tuck" affair. Pulled about by competing emotional loyalties and discordant versions of reality, such persons were subjected to intense emotional strain. (p. 873)

In our profiles, this can be seen most clearly in the complexities of Don's relationships; it is also well documented in the literature. For some of our profile adults, however, emotional attachments are a source of support and the "incipient transformation" is viewed as a positive, desirable change. Relationships can provide a sense of security and predictability, a resource that can be drawn on in the change process. Even in these situations, however, interpersonal dynamics can be a source of stress; change is difficult, no matter how positive. Learners may be concerned about the impact on their social networks, particularly when they have been exchanging their skills and knowledge with adults who offer assistance with literacy. For example, if a woman's husband has been the primary reader, she may worry about his feeling displaced if she begins to read for herself; the balance of exchange is altered.

All students experience some change in their interpersonal relationships when their literacy practices change, depending on the extent to which they previously had assistance with tasks that they are doing independently now, or the extent to which they involve others in new tasks (see Fingeret, 1983; Ziegahn, 1990). Change also occurs as a result of changes in self-definition and inner confidence. For example, Marsha sees herself moving beyond her old crowd. She has a vision of her life that no longer includes their ways of spending time. Her relationship with herself is changing as she learns to use writing to develop her self-awareness. Lawrence's friends are supportive, although they recognize that he doesn't need them in the ways that he used to. Ann doesn't ask her daughter for help as often as she used to. Don resists changes in relationships and lifestyle by acting as though he is unable to engage in some literacy practices that actually are within his ability.

The larger literature base includes examples of marriages that dissolve as well as students who quit programs due to the stress of participation on relationships. Because we chose our profile participants on other bases, we do not have these examples in the group of profiled adults; such examples can be found elsewhere in the literature, however (see, for example, Fingeret, 1982).

The distinction between insiders and outsiders is not clear; persons outside the program may share many of the beliefs of those inside the program, including belief in someone's ability to learn and in their inherent worth and dignity. The distinction between relationships with those inside and outside the program in our cases has more to do with the impact of change. Those inside the program are sharing in the learning process; the relationships are new, and are established through the learning and changing process.

Those outside the program already have established ways of interacting with the student around literacy. These relationships must change, and we can assume that the dynamics of change will cover a broad spectrum. In some cases, these relationships will be a source of assistance and support, helping to overcome shame and engage in new practices. In other instances, these relationships may be so resistant to change that the student leaves the literacy program rather than further endanger the relationship or, in some cases, personal safety.

Learning is central to the changes that are taking place in relationships; it is important to recognize the centrality of effective instruction in this process of growth and change. On one level, adults are learning about themselves and are changing their notions of what is possible for them. But on another level, adults are learning the technical aspects of literacy, and putting that together with their cultural and social knowledge to develop the capacity to engage in new literacy practices. LVNYC fosters these outcomes through an instructional approach that provides multiple opportunities for engaging in literacy practices and for experiencing literacy as a social process. By approaching literacy as a process of constructing meaning, LVNYC incorporates students' preexisting knowledge and experience into the instructional process. Emphasizing writing as well as reading, LVNYC helps learners develop their own voice as well as gain access to all the voices that are already in print.

Adults assess the potential for effectiveness in an instructional program while engaging in problem solving and seeking. Moving through the latter aspects of the change process requires that learning is taking place; practices must begin to change. At first, new practices can be expected primarily inside the program. Students are learning to spell and decode, to write their names and their stories, and to read the newspaper's account of the accident they witnessed on their way to work that day. They are learning that they like some authors better than others, that they feel more comfortable writing about some topics than about others, and that they can critique others' writing as well as improve their own. They are learning that they can look back over a body of work for the previous six months and tell some things about their progress.

All of this learning inside the program contributes to changes in practices outside the program, which in turn drive changes in relationships that support and stimulate learning. Change is taking place inside and outside the program simultaneously; relationships and new practices inside the program provide a foundation for change outside, and adults bring back into the program experience with literacy outside. As this happens, students are pushing and redefining the boundaries between inside and outside, between public and private situations.

We can think of the movement from inside to outside, and from private to public, as movement across *boundaries*. As in any social system, the boundaries change as people and situations change. Sometimes the boundary-crossings feel like major changes, such as the first time an adult actually engages in any new literacy practice outside the program. At other times the boundaries are pushed, rather than crossed, as part of a process of moving on the continuum to engage in practices that are progressively more public and feel more standardized.

Sometimes learners try to engage in new literacy practices, crossing new boundaries, but find that they "go blank," as shame and performance anxiety interfere. This particularly may happen in situations that feel more public or with practices that have little flexibility, such as using an automatic teller machine (ATM). With support and experience, these practices may become familiar and anxiety may recede.

At other times, however, learners may not be willing to try new practices because the shame is too intense. They may be unwilling to expose their literacy practices to the scrutiny of strangers or even to their own judgment of adequate performance in certain situations. Often students who can describe important and concrete positive changes in their abilities, self-concept, self-esteem, and practices nonetheless also say that they still have not told many of their friends, family members, employers, and co-workers about the limits to their literacy practices, their participation in a literacy program, or their newly emerging abilities.

Every boundary is an opportunity for growth and learning; every boundary-crossing requires courage and invokes issues of shame, in differing degrees. As learners become more skilled and confident, their definitions of literacy in specific situations may begin to change, their demands on their own performance may shift, and their general feeling of vulnerability in public situations may decrease. Banks, grocery stores, public transportation, and jobs may lose some of their associations with danger, shame, and stress. And students will continue to seek environments and resources that support their efforts at crossing boundaries.

For example, Lawrence and Marsha challenge themselves all the time; they move between inside and outside the program, developing confidence in situations that feel private to push themselves into situations that feel increasingly public. Lawrence began writing inside the program, in a situation that felt private. He started sharing his writing with family and friends outside the program, in situations that felt private. Then he read his writing to a group of 40 persons—a situation that felt more public, but inside the program. Now he is using the automatic teller machine—a literacy practice outside the program in a situation that feels quite public. Lawrence keeps moving between domains and pushing boundaries.

Lawrence and Marsha are excited by their new literacy practices. They describe their progress and learning in terms of new achievements and the contexts in which those achievements are meaningful. They also describe a new relationship with themselves. Marsha talks about her writing as an inner dialog through which she is coming to know herself; Lawrence talks about his comfort with staying home to write, rather than going out and staying busy.

Intensive Continuing Interaction

Maria experiments with new literacy practices in many arenas in her life, including but not limited to her instructional small group. Although Maria wants to become more independent through literacy, she also views literacy fundamentally as a social process. She engages her entire family in literacy practices on a regular basis, emphasizing collaboration and community rather than personal achievement. Maria brings her sense of "family" to her tutoring group; she enjoys the interaction and mutual support that typifies her experience with group instruction. Maria and Lawrence, in particular, feel that group instruction helps to increase their confidence; they often help others and their progress is recognized by the group. They struggle with issues of interpersonal dynamics and power relationships within the group. Success within a group reinforces risk-taking. Each successfully negotiated boundary encourages crossing another.

Maria found in her tutoring group what she was familiar with at home among family—people working together, supporting one another, accepting each other, sharing knowledge, talents, and skills. She creates private situations inside and outside the program in which she feels safe to try new literacy practices. She and her children teach each other and learn together without shame or embarrassment; Maria's tutoring group benefits from her knowledge of interdependence that is rooted in her family experience. Maria's increasing confidence allows her to keep pushing the boundaries of public and private, transforming threatening situations into opportunities for practice. Maria's husband is supportive of the changes in her relationships with her family; he is ill now and can no longer do all of the literacy practices required in the family. Her developing literacy abilities help to keep the family together. Maria is engaged in a profound transformation (Mezirow, 1991, 1996) as she learns about herself and the possibilities in her life at the same time she develops new literacy practices. Lawrence also carries some group dynamics skills outside, as we see when he talks about speaking up at work.

Broad change requires this kind of *intensive interaction*. We see that Maria engages in new literacy practices at home, out in the world, and in the program. She spends a lot of time with her children and her husband engaged in literacy activities. She is coming to see herself as someone who can and does use literacy for information as well as entertainment. She has begun helping others develop their literacy abilities and she is involved in her children's schooling. The literacy program provides an opportunity for her to develop relationships with other adults who validate her new identity and support her continuing change.

Our data show that adults who experience the deepest and most profound life change, such as Maria and, to a lesser extent, Lawrence, engage in new literacy practices in both public and private situations. They engage with print as individuals, as parents, as workers, and as members of their community. Reading and writing become more than a set of skills or tasks practiced in a literacy program; they become tools these individuals actively use to bring about the quality of life they desire. Don, Ann, and Marsha engage in new literacy practices in a much more limited way, often continuing to separate themselves from many family, friends, and co-workers as well as remaining leery of public literacy practices.

Shame is central to movement between inside and outside, and affects as well as being affected by relationships on both sides of the boundaries. Authors agree that coming out of hiding and developing genuine, caring friendships are important early steps in healing shame (Goldberg, 1991; Kaufman, 1985). This includes relationships inside as well as outside of the program.

Intensive interaction inside the literacy program provides opportunities for the development of relationships that mediate the sense of shame and isolation and help adults integrate literacy into their identities. As adults experience success with learning and listen to the similarities between their stories and those of their fellow students, they may begin to develop a more critical perspective on literacy and literacy development.

Placing their experience in a broader framework and seeing the extent to which social and political conditions share responsibility for their problems with literacy can begin to mediate self-blame.

As students' abilities to engage in literacy practices develop, their image of themselves may move closer to their ideal and their self-esteem may increase. In addition, increased self-esteem may be fostered through experiencing themselves successfully relating well to others, including college-educated volunteers and staff members; helping others, as seen in their interaction in their groups; and writing pieces that others find worthy of publishing. As a result, the negative feelings students have about their relationship to literacy may have a smaller impact on their general self-esteem. In addition, basic self-concept begins to change as adults begin to view themselves as writers and readers.

We have been focusing on viewing literacy as practices; there is an important role for literacy as critical reflection and action as well. Adults' sense of shame is rooted in their childhood experiences as well as in the criteria they hold for "good" performance. As students' criteria change and their analysis becomes more structural and sophisticated, adults can begin to transform the underlying basis on which judgments of esteem are calculated; their perspectives can change, decreasing the power of other people's judgments on their performance.

Bradshaw (1988), Kaufman (1985), and Goldberg (1991) describe a number of psychotherapeutic models for addressing self-blame and shame in general. Atkins, Day, Shore, & Simon (1990) describe a process of integrating counseling and literacy instruction specifically to help learners develop a critical perspective on our society's structural inequalities. Atkins et al. argue that the social myths of equal opportunity are internalized, fueling adults' beliefs that their lack of success in the schooling system must be their own fault, even though poverty, racism, sexism, and classism often play central roles. Therefore, Atkins et al. claim, "the exposure of social myths becomes a critical element in overcoming many of the internal barriers to learning" (p. 13).

For example, some students believe that they cannot participate in more extensive literacy practices because they are "stupid" and had been unable to learn when they had the chance in public schools. By explicitly exploring the sources of these beliefs, students may be able to place their own efforts in relation to the constraints of poverty, racism, and other sociocultural conditions that may have affected their learning. As a result, students may "begin the process of transforming their meaning perspectives as part of the process of gaining greater control over their lives as learners and as participants in that social process" (Atkins et al., 1990, p. 4). As the sense of self-blame decreases and self-concept shifts, students may be able to risk engaging in new literacy practices that had felt unattainable previously.

Mezirow (1991) describes this kind of perspective transformation:

> Perspective transformation is the process of becoming critically aware of how and why our presuppositions have come to constrain the way we perceive, understand, and feel about our world; of reformulating these assumptions to permit a more inclusive, discriminating, permeable, and integrative perspective; and of making decisions or otherwise acting upon these new understandings. (p. 14)

Perspective transformation is far more broadly applicable than simply examining shame; it is central to the process of adults' moving into an identity as literate persons, with literacy practices integrated into their lives. This transformation appears to incorporate intensive interaction both inside and outside the program.

Intensive interaction outside the literacy program provides opportunities for adults to construct their images and meanings of literacy practices from the larger society—they watch people who are literate, they listen to how people talk about reading and writing, they remember their own public school teachers, and they notice how other people respond to them in a variety of situations. Each literacy practice comes with some sense of norms attached to it, or a sense of how it is done in the situation. These constructed norms—the ways that adults expect their literacy practices to be judged by others—provide the framework within which adults judge themselves as literate, or judge their progress toward literacy. They can also reinforce a sense of shame and differentness. Ferdman (1990) explains, "To be literate it is not enough, for example, to know how to sign one's name. One must also know when and where it is appropriate to do so. Reading and writing behaviors must be done in the 'right' way" (p. 187).

Literacy practices vary in the extent to which they are constrained by the expectations of the larger society. For example, some literacy practices may be perceived as having few norms and a sense of great personal flexibility about participation in the situation, such as making a birthday card for a dear friend. Other literacy practices, however, are extensively standardized; there are norms regarding body language, speed and accuracy, and vocabulary as well as technical skills. For example, many adults in New York City have watched people reading in subway trains, and they have identified norms for this practice. As a result, when they want to read while riding on the subway, they often believe that they must not move their lips or subvocalize, that the pages should be turned in certain intervals, and that the reading material should be held in a certain way. They may decide not to read rather than to read in ways that do not conform to these images.

Engaging in literacy practices in private situations reduces anxiety because it involves different norms and does not leave someone vulnerable to the judgment of strangers and the general public. In public situations, however, the stigma that was worn on the inside—difficulty with literacy—has to be exposed to the world. Adults feel that they will be judged against a set of norms they had no voice in creating. This anxiety about norms fuels the sense of shame.

When students engage in new literacy practices, they are also engaging in a profound process of reconstructing their definitions of normal and their relationship to the dominant culture. Once the deep sense of shame begins to abate, anxiety over performance changes as well. This facilitates moving across boundaries, from inside to outside the program, from private to public situations, and from practices that feel more flexible to those that feel more standardized. The courage to engage in intensive interaction is essential to this movement.

SECTION III

Implications for Programs and Practice

Adults come to literacy programs as actors rather than as passive receivers of services. In many cases they have persevered through numerous difficulties including previous experiences with programs that did not meet their needs; problems arranging child care, work schedules, or transportation; family attitudes that were unsupportive of additional education; or personal fears about meeting strangers and taking tests. Adults who make it to literacy programs are pushing boundaries because they want to engage in new literacy practices that will help them to change their lives in some way. They may want to read to their children, qualify for a supervisor's job, accept leadership roles in civic organizations, read the Bible, write letters to old friends, and so on.

Adult literacy program staff and volunteers must be equipped to help learners with the complex issues that arise in relation to change. This includes helping learners consider the "costs" of developing new literacy practices. It also includes helping learners draw on the personal resources that they bring to the change process and providing a curriculum that directly addresses learners' interests and circumstances outside the program. Many literacy programs, however, provide a curriculum that is oriented to success in schooling rather than success in the world outside. Workbooks and other texts often reflect knowledge and behaviors that are valued primarily by educators and mainstream white, middle-class culture. Educators often make assumptions about what their students "need" to learn or "should" learn, without appropriate consultation with students.

The framework for change we presented in Section II suggests that adult literacy programs can become more intentional about helping students move through the process of changing their lives. In Section III we explore these implications of the framework for practitioners. This includes asking practitioners to become more reflective about their philosophy of education and their values, and to view literacy education as a partnership with their students. This, in turn, has implications for instruction and curriculum development. Program practices have to support new approaches to instruction and curriculum, and we particularly emphasize the need for new ways of evaluating learner progress and program effectiveness.

10

The Process of Change

In order to explore the implications of our framework, we consulted directly with adult students and their literacy teachers. In a series of workshop sessions we brought adult students and teachers together to share their own stories of learning and change. After much discussion of the issues arising from these stories, we invited participants to critique our framework for change. We asked if they thought our framework reflected their stories and overwhelmingly they said yes; they were able to recognize themselves and people they knew. We then asked these students and teachers what could be done by adult literacy programs to help students move through the process of changing their daily literacy practices and develop identities as literate people. Specifically, we wanted to know what programs might anticipate at various points in the framework and how they could respond to students in ways that would support their change efforts. Participants' responses were both insightful and consistent, reflecting rich experience as consumers and providers of literacy services.

Prolonged Tension and Turning Points

Both teachers and students talk about the need for programs to recognize the sources of tension and dissatisfaction that propel adults into literacy programs. They speak of the importance of both counseling and instruction and of the usefulness of maintaining community resource networks linking social service agencies and program participants. Learners suggest that peer support groups be immediately available to students when they enter a new program. In support groups, students can share their ways of coping with problems outside with adults who have had similar experiences. Teachers can admit to learners, as they did in one workshop, that "we do this every day and we forget the tensions that you all are experiencing. We do it so much we lose sight of that." Learners can remind their teachers that it is not just the problems outside that create tension, but that coming back to school as an adult is frightening and stressful in and of itself.

Entering a literacy program for the first time represents one kind of boundary-crossing. The fear of crossing this boundary is only partially directed at the actual problems of engaging in new literacy practices. Often the larger issue is the fear of exposure, of feeling shamed again, of experiencing the unique pain of humiliation. Through counseling, students can be taught constructive ways of responding to negative self-talk, such as simple relaxation exercises. They can be encouraged to discharge their shame and fear, allowing more positive emotions to develop. Counseling may help students transform their feelings of self-blame and deal with other issues in their lives.

Where possible, adult literacy programs should make counseling services available to students in a variety of formats. This could include providing students with the training and support they need to function as peer counselors and offering counseling services to students at program sites in private offices. Counselors also can be available as a resource to help teachers and tutors better understand the dynamics of their experience and develop skills to work with students more effectively.

Each of the students in our profiles talks about the comfort they find in meeting other students who are "like them" and the importance of discovering they are not alone as people who experience literacy problems. The students with whom we consulted in our workshops agree that if new students could be oriented to the program by experienced students when they first arrive, this would help alleviate some of the initial fear.

The turning point that frees someone to consider a literacy program may also entail a loss of income or the need for child care. It may raise questions about identity as a student struggles with a divorce or the death of someone close. Relationships with friends and family members outside the program may begin to fragment as student's priorities for their time change. Students often get scared, worried about losing the security of their social networks and the security of their old ways of being in the world. Trusting relationships inside the program can help students compensate for some of the loss experienced outside the program. The students we spoke with emphasized the importance of a comfortable classroom environment. One student said, "It helps to be like a family. . . . This motivates people to stay." Teachers we spoke with told us they see the need to create bonding among students and staff and to create an environment that is "warm and welcoming, not judgmental."

Adults in literacy programs need opportunities to talk with each other about their shame, their literacy, and their feelings, in order to develop trusting relationships with other students and staff. This important initial trust can help students cross boundaries from private into increasingly public situations. As adults begin to view themselves as writers and readers inside the program, the distance between their desired and actual self-concept begins to decrease, thus sustaining the courage to cross boundaries and transform the prolonged sense of shame and self-blame.

Uncertainty about the literacy program they are considering compounds the tension in students' lives. Students told us, "People would come back to school if they knew what it was all about." Another reminded us, "When you walk in there, you're in a different environment. You don't know what's what." Adult literacy programs should affirm students' identities as problem solvers and help position them as knowledgeable consumers of the services.

Problem Solving and Seeking Educational Opportunities

To be active, knowledgeable consumers of literacy services students tell us they need to know what programs are available and specifically what those programs have to offer. Most students said that more adults would take advantage of literacy services if these services were advertised more extensively and in a variety of ways, such as using former students to promote programs and advertising in places where adults are likely to go. If literacy programs maintain a higher visibility in their communities and make clear what goes on inside them, friends and family members might feel less threatened when they start attending. For example, an "open house" could be held so that friends and family could come and see for themselves what goes on in a literacy program. In addition, adults who seek out programs with particular goals in mind want to know in advance that programs are set up to help them meet those goals. Programs could have an orientation day so that adults could be sure they had made the right program choice. This would also help them cope with their apprehension about entering a new situation.

Once the decision is made to enter a program, students continue to monitor whether their needs are being met. Both Lawrence and Maria, for instance, find that the relationships they develop through group instruction at LVNYC help to sustain their involvement. Lawrence and Marsha agree that writing about their lives and receiving help in a supportive environment make their involvement worthwhile. For Don, working one-on-one with a responsive and fairly "demanding" tutor is important. He also wants to know that his tutor will be the same one next time. Ann values the program for its supportive social environment.

The students with whom we consulted in workshop sessions affirmed that they, too, come to understand the conditions inside a program that help them learn. They suggest that program staff consult with new students to talk about what they know about their own learning, and that staff involve all students in examining their progress toward their goals and how that progress relates to the instructional program. This suggests that programs might involve everyone—students, tutors, and staff—in reexamining the models of leadership and decision making that are implicit in their work. Participatory approaches to planning and evaluating literacy programs would bring together various perspectives, leading to renewed energy around the program, enhanced learning for everyone, and substantive progress toward change in areas central to students' lives.

Some students, like Ann, remain hesitant to speak out about conditions inside the program because they do not feel it is within their right or they do not want to criticize people who are doing "the best they can." It is important to examine students' tension between feeling grateful to program staff, particularly volunteers, and feeling that some of their tutors or teachers are inadequately skilled. Reluctance to criticize may be connected to students' feelings of shame. As marginalized persons, students overcome great emotional obstacles to ask for help and deal with their pride when they are receiving free services. This is a problem to the extent that it interferes with students' providing open and honest feedback to program staff about the effectiveness of their instruction; it denies students their role as active participants in creating change in their lives. Affirming students' identities as consumers of literacy services means creating an environment in which their concerns about the instructional program are encouraged and openly addressed with respect.

Changing Relationships and Changing Practices:
Inside and Outside the Program

The curriculum has to address students' outside interests and concerns, looking at students as complete adults rather than compartmentalizing their lives. This does not always occur; one teacher told us, "We spend so much time focusing on the academics because we think that's what we're here for and what we need to do is realize that there's more to it." Students with whom we spoke told us that they would like the curriculum focused around problems they face outside the program. They talked about the need for instruction in how to handle stress and relationship conflicts. They said they would like reading material that addresses single parenthood, goal setting and life planning, fears of change, and what it means to become more independent. Also, Maria appreciated that her tutor shared his outside life with the group; both teachers and learners can bring the outside into the classroom.

When the curriculum is oriented to tasks, even if they are similar to those found outside the program, all too often it becomes another burden to bear rather than providing a source of additional support or assistance. This occurs when the social and cultural context is ignored. When the focus is on tasks rather than practices, the curriculum remains firmly inside the program.

> Authentic activities are most simply defined as the ordinary practices of the culture. . . . When authentic activities are transferred to the classroom, their context is inevitably transmuted; they become classroom tasks and part of the school culture. . . . In the creation of classroom tasks, apparently peripheral features of authentic tasks—like the extralinguistic supports involved in the interpretation of communication—are often dismissed as "noise" from which salient features can be abstracted for the purpose of teaching. But the context of activity is an extraordinarily complex network from which practitioners draw essential support. . . . At the same time, students may come to rely, in important but little noticed ways, on features of the classroom context, in which the task is now embedded, that are wholly absent from and alien to authentic activity. Thus, much of what is learned in school may apply only to the ersatz activity. (Brown, Collins, & Duguid, 1989, p. 34)

Exercises in which students fill in sample job application forms, for example, or compare prices in the grocery store ads in the daily newspaper, only simulate the practices in their lives. As long as they remain inside the program, these practices cannot duplicate the social and cultural demands that adults feel outside the program, particularly in public situations. The students we talked to appreciate this difference between practicing technical literacy skills and tasks inside the program and engaging in practices outside.

Students can help program staff better reproduce some of the peripheral features of practices that are anxiety-producing on the outside, such as time limits and noise. But students also said that they would like more opportunity to go outside the program, with other students and staff, to practice in real situations. They told us that it would be helpful to use the ATM machine for the first time, write checks at the grocery store, or try out the computers at the library in the company of other students and their teachers. This is similar to learning apprenticeships or supervised practica prevalent in many other adult learning programs. We do not expect medical students to move directly to practice without supervision and the assistance of peers.

The organization of work inside the program can help support pushing boundaries outside as well. In traditional education, school learning is primarily individual and judgments are made of individual achievement.

However, Resnick (1987) claims that "in contrast, much activity outside school is socially shared. . . . Each person's ability to function successfully depends on what others do and how several individuals' mental and physical performances mesh" (p. 13). Resnick examines programs that effectively teach thinking skills and higher-order cognitive abilities and finds that they share many characteristics with out-of-school cognitive activity. Resnick explains in more detail:

> First, most of the effective programs have features characteristic of out-of-school cognitive performances. They involve socially shared intellectual work, and they are organized around joint accomplishment of tasks, so that elements of the skill take on meaning in the context of the whole. Second, many of the programs have elements of apprenticeship. That is, they make usually hidden processes overt, and they encourage student observation and commentary. They also allow skill to build up bit by bit, yet permit participation even for the relatively unskilled, often as a result of the social sharing of tasks. Finally, the most successful programs are organized around particular bodies of knowledge and interpretation—subject matters if you will—rather than general abilities. (p. 18)

Group instruction, development of a sense of community, and development of relevant curriculum are examples of ways that programs like LVNYC can facilitate students' movement and change.

Instruction also can contribute to transforming students' self-blame, particularly when coupled with counseling. Atkins et al. (1990) provide numerous concrete examples of what it looks like to incorporate this kind of critical analysis into group instruction. They have piloted a model in which a counselor is in the classroom with the teacher. Their model emphasizes helping students to understand the role of structural inequality, racism, sexism, and classism, "through the process of validation of feelings, exposure of social myths, reframing experiences and helping students to act to gain greater control in and out of the classroom. Addressing issues of self-blame is a key factor in empowerment" (p. 46). Auerbach (1992), Nash, Cason, Rhum, McGrail, & Gomez-Sanford (1992), and Shor (1987) provide additional examples of what this kind of education looks like.

When programs fail to recognize the importance of helping students move into increasingly public situations, adult learners are left to struggle on their own to move their new practices from inside to outside the program. Although students may have developed new technical skills, practices, and confidence in their ability inside the program, old feelings of shame and fear of embarrassment reemerge as they consider moving into more public situations. The costs associated with trying literacy practices outside the program may seem too high for many students. Shame, embarrassment, and fear of public humiliation create new boundaries that some students choose not to cross.

On the other hand, when students have the opportunity to interact with literate persons, they begin to see them in a more realistic light. They learn that experienced readers don't know every word and that they too misspell words. Their willingness to take risks with new literacy practices is increased; their enjoyment of literacy is enhanced. When students begin interacting with literate persons inside and outside the program as they increase their own repertoire of literacy practices, other relationships in their lives begin to shift. Recognizing this, the students we spoke with emphasized again the importance of strong peer support and counseling inside the program as well as help coping with the interpersonal conflict that can arise when friends and family feel threatened by the new situation.

Intensive Continuing Interaction

Although educators often refer to "application," engaging in new literacy practices is really new learning—taking knowledge and skills developed in one social and cultural context, such as the classroom, and applying them in a new social and cultural context, such as a grocery store. Even though the technical literacy abilities may be the same in both instances, additional knowledge and skill about the norms of the task in the new setting and new meanings that relate to specific contexts are necessary also. Sometimes these differences reflect class boundaries; learners' aspirations of social mobility require a kind of cross-cultural education. The final condition, intensive interaction, refers to contact in the diverse social and cultural contexts that exist both inside and outside the program. Culture is central to the concept of practices as we have discussed it here; literacy education is cross-cultural on a number of dimensions. Learners are attempting to cross boundaries from predominately oral to more literate culture, as well as crossing boundaries of race and class.

Teachers' or tutors' cultural background often differs significantly from that of their students in adult literacy programs. Ellsworth (1989) writes persuasively about the difficulties of this kind of teaching assignment, in the context of her own experience. As an "Anglo, middle-class professor," as she labels herself, "there are things that I as professor could never know about the experiences, oppressions and understandings of other participants in the class" (p. 310).

When cultural differences associated with race, class, and gender are present in literacy programs, this provides an opportunity for students and teachers to explore the implications of cultural differences existing outside the program. At the same time, when the gap is very pronounced, aggressive steps should be taken to increase the cultural diversity of staff and volunteers. Education in cross-cultural communication can be included in the curriculum as well as in staff development. Both students and staff can benefit from assistance in recognizing and understanding issues of race, culture, gender, dialect, and class differences that arise both inside and outside the program. Students who make deep and pervasive changes in their literacy practices and in their identities as literate people interact increasingly with other literate persons in diverse social and cultural contexts. Adult literacy programs can develop ways to support students' engaging in literacy practices in situations that are increasingly public. For example, some literacy programs include activities that involve people students do not know well or who are not inside the programs, such as award and graduation ceremonies, or talking with the media. Since these activities are connected to the feeling of support that comes from being inside the program, these public events often are considered "inside." Public situations inside the program also include students' speaking to groups of new tutors or teachers, or reading out loud at a ceremony or celebration; the program creates a sense of safety that supports new public literacy practices.

Although public, these situations retain the feeling of being inside, among one's friends and peers. Such occasions act as a bridge between inside and outside the program; there is a certain predictability and sense of control as well as a public commitment to value personal practices. At the same time, these occasions invite a carefully selected group of people, such as friends, kin, and new teachers. New readers and new writers know that these persons know about their struggles with literacy. Students do not have to worry about managing the information in this setting; these people are on "their side."

11

Evaluation of Learning

Students' progress in literacy programs traditionally has been evaluated by the administration of standardized reading tests such as the Adult Basic Learning Examination (ABLE), the Test of Adult Basic Education (TABE—Reading subtest), or the Degree of Reading Power Test (DRP). At LVNYC during the period of the original study, these were administered to students during the Preenrollment Program (PEP) and thereafter at 50-hour intervals. These tests are based on a definition of literacy as technical skills or tasks; they do not assess the extent to which students engage in new literacy practices. On a more informal basis, tutors met with students to review and discuss progress toward student-identified goals.

For the original study we examined standardized test score differences over time, when the scores were available, and we analyzed a series of writing samples from each student (see Appendix for more discussion of methodology). The writing samples provided some indication of changes in practices, but remained firmly inside the program. In most instances students decided on their writing topics; students had no control over the content of the standardized test questions. We also interviewed friends and family members, in some cases.

All of the students in the profiles believe they are developing their ability to participate more extensively in literacy practices through their participation in Literacy Volunteers of New York City. Their assessment is supported strongly by their narratives, our interviews with their family and friends, and an analysis of their writing samples. However, it is supported in a much weaker fashion, or sometimes not at all, by analysis of the standardized test scores.

An emphasis on literacy as practices raises questions about the usefulness of standardized testing for providing relevant information about student learning. The framework we present in Section II can provide guidance for developing alternative approaches to assessing student progress and evaluating program effectiveness.

Comparing Test Scores, Writing Samples, and Testimony

Lawrence's standardized test scores at entry into the program were a little above the fourth-grade level; he has been in the program 7 months and has no second set of standardized test scores. In our analysis of Lawrence's writing samples, we find that in the 6-month interval between his samples, there has been an 8-point improvement. He showed improvement particularly in the areas of (1) vocabulary and (2) content and organization for meaning. This suggests that his writing has become easier to follow, better organized, and more expressive.

Lawrence assesses his improvement by also looking at practices; he says he is filling in applications, reading books, using dictionaries, planning a vacation, reading to his sister's children, communicating more easily in general, speaking to groups in the program, and learning how to type from a book. He also talks a lot about how much he enjoys writing stories.

Don's last standardized reading test score was a month below his grade-equivalent entry level of first grade, sixth month; his standardized test scores have actually decreased over time. Don is a prolific writer and has been published by LVNYC. He turned in 22 writing samples for this evaluation and showed a 13-point improvement in two samples over an 18-month interval. This suggests substantial improvement in the clarity, expressiveness, and organization of his writing.

Don talks about how his relationships have changed, particularly with his brother and his mother. He is not afraid to take public transportation any more and he lists many daily-life tasks that he is doing for the first time, including getting a telephone and managing the bill, buying clothes and groceries on his own, and paying some of the household bills. Don feels that he made good progress in reading in his first group assignment, but that he is not continuing to make progress now.

Maria entered the program testing above the fourth-grade level on her standardized reading test. She jokes about the ruses she uses to get out of taking the test at the appropriate intervals; she has been successful, since there are no second test scores for her, although she has been in the program for more than 7 months, which is well beyond the 50-hour interval. Maria's writing score improved 13 points in the first 7 months she was in the program, according to our analysis of her writing samples. Improvements were noted across all the areas of writing, indicating more sophisticated writing generally, with increased organization, coherence, expressiveness, and correct use of punctuation.

Maria discusses improvement in reading and writing by describing practices she couldn't do before, such as writing checks, reading and writing more independently, talking about things she is reading, performing literacy tasks on her job more independently, helping her friends and neighbors with their literacy development, and helping her children with their schoolwork. Improvement in reading and writing means changes in how Maria feels about herself and how she relates to her children and husband. Maria says that her enjoyment of writing has increased enormously; she used to hate it and now she cannot write fast enough to get all of her ideas down. Maria's husband and two of her children were interviewed and they strongly corroborated her assessment of her learning.

Students in the original study realize that the standardized tests provide information about their "level" in order to get into the program and that grade levels have something to do with leaving the program. Other than that, they do not consider the standardized tests relevant or useful in letting them know how they are doing in the program. Students do not use test scores to inform themselves of their own improvement in reading or writing; rather, they talk about new literacy practices or accomplishments, such as books they have read. Lawrence and Maria do not have second test scores but they are very articulate about their learning. Don's decreasing score might actually be understood as a reflection of his learning:

> It is possible . . . that negative gain may occur because learners on the pre-test do not work at any given item too long, because they think they cannot perform the test task, and so they simply guess at all the items. On the post-test they spend more time on each item because they have new competence and think they should not guess but try to actually comprehend and perform each item. This could lead to more accurate, but fewer test items being completed at the post-test, and hence a negative gain score. (Sticht, 1990, p. 21)

Lawrence, Don, and Maria illustrate some of the shortcomings of using standardized tests for assessment of learning; even their writing samples provide only one part of the complex picture of change in practices.

Alternatives to Standardized Testing

As programs become more oriented to literacy practices, there is an increasing distance between the instruction and the assumptions inherent in the standardized tests. Lytle and Wolfe (1989) explain:

> There is often a wide gulf between the instruction provided in a program and what is assessed in a standardized test. . . . Sometimes it is a struggle for learners to see the relationship between a multifaceted curriculum and progress as determined by a standardized test. . . . Still further, the format of

standardized tests as collections of passages with questions that have single right answers demonstrates a view of reading that denies the possibility of multiple readings of texts or of texts read for a variety of purposes. (p. 45)

The students participating in this study are engaged in literacy practices in which the subskills and tasks are embedded in social relationships that occur in a variety of situations. Their concern is being able to function in those situations in new ways. There are well-documented problems with standardized testing (see D'Amico-Samuels, 1991; Ehringhaus 1991; Farr & Carey, 1986; Wrigley & Guth, 1992). Our concern here is with the extent to which it does not reflect the students' changes in participation in literacy practices. Most notably, the subskills and tasks measured by the standardized tests do not indicate the extent to which students are able to change their literacy practices. In addition, since practices are social, these shifts imply changes in relationships as well, which are not captured.

"Authentic assessment" is the term broadly used to describe approaches to assessment that involve reflection on and analysis of a sample of artifacts from literacy practices drawn from many domains in students' lives. Portfolio assessment is one example of authentic assessment that is becoming increasingly widespread in adult literacy education programs (see Fingeret, 1993); it has the potential to counteract many of the limitations of standardized testing.

Portfolio assessment means many things these days; we offer portfolio assessment as an approach to assessment that is consistent with viewing literacy as practices. A portfolio is a folder in which students keep a sample of the larger body of their literacy work, including artifacts of their literacy practices outside the literacy program such as copies of driver's licenses, copies of the title pages of books that parents read to their children, copies of letters written to friends and family, and examples of math, reading, and writing done in church, civic association meetings, or on the job. These are known as presentation or showcase portfolios (Tierney, Carter, & Desai, 1991). The portfolio, which is the content as well as the folder, can be diverse, as Valencia (1990) explains:

> The range of items to include in a portfolio is almost limitless but may include written responses to reading, reading logs, selected daily work, pieces of writing at various stages of completion, classroom tests, checklists, unit projects, and audio or video tapes, to name a few. The key is to ensure a variety of types of indicators of learning so that teachers, . . . students, and administrators can build a complete picture of the student's development. (p. 339)

Portfolios also can include copies of journal pages in which students discuss their learning.

The portfolio's contents are drawn from a larger collection of materials that has been kept in folders or other kinds of containers. Students develop criteria about what they want to transfer from the larger collection (Paulson, Paulson, & Meyer, 1991) and analyze their work as they select and move different pieces. Students discuss their analysis and choices with other students and with their teachers, getting other perspectives on their learning and growth and reviewing the concrete evidence of their movement.

Portfolio assessment is not easy, but there are many rewards:

> Portfolios are messy. They demand intimate and often frighteningly subjective talk with students. Portfolios are work. . . . What comes out of portfolio-based assessment? The immediate answer lies in integrity and the validity of the information we gain about how and what students learn. But that's far from all. (Wolf, 1989, p. 37)

Fingeret (1993) interviewed literacy practitioners and students who were using portfolio assessment. Her findings support the claims made in the literature (see, for example, Wolf, 1989) that portfolio assessment helps students learn to reflect on what they've learned and how they learn, reinforces and broadens students' understanding of what they've learned, and supports practitioners' continuing learning and development.

Assessment has to be many-faceted, reflecting the needs of learners, practitioners, funders, and policymakers. However, the framework presented here, the voices of the learners in our profiles, and the larger literature base in adult literacy education all demand an assessment process that helps students portray and reflect on the extent to which literacy education is helping them make real changes in they way they live their lives, day by day.

The Framework as a Tool

As one of the literacy practitioners was leaving the workshop in which she had discussed the implications of this framework for change, she said, "We already know that these things need to be done. But we don't do them." Indeed, many of the suggestions in the previous chapter are being implemented in many programs. Practitioners and students are working together to improve instruction and to make programs more responsive to learners' characteristics and situations. And we see most of the program and instructional suggestions in the literature already (see, for example, Beder, 1991; Fingeret, 1992; Soifer et al., 1990).

At the same time, however, many programs continue as they have for the last 30 years; change is difficult and comes slowly. Resources have been decreasing, which has placed an added burden on already overextended teachers and administrators. Policymakers have sometimes viewed literacy programs as serving relatively narrow ends, such as increased employment, making it difficult at times for practitioners to be fully responsive to students. In addition, problems that have plagued the field historically continue, in most cases. These include a dearth of full-time employment and career opportunities for practitioners, inadequate facilities, unstable funding, limited conceptualization of and access to professional development opportunities, marginalization, and isolation.

The challenge faced by the literacy field right now is to develop a unified vision that supports change. Stein (1997, p. 1) explains:

> For too long, we have approached adult literacy and basic skills education as if its purpose is to make up for something adults didn't get in the past. Now we know that its purpose is to prepare adults for the future—to build on what they have already learned through experience as well as formal education, to prepare them for new, unimagined responsibilities in the present, and to provide them with the tools to enable them to continue to learn. In short, the task before adult educators today is to equip their students for the future.

We hope that the framework we suggest will assist in expanding the dialogue between students and practitioners to generate new ideas, and improve our understanding of the importance of counseling, peer support groups, and relevant instruction. Working together, practitioners and students can turn problems into opportunities, responding to pressures in new ways rather than retreating into old patterns. For example, one teacher at a workshop responded to students' requests for program orientation by talking about her program's decreased number of staff members. As a result, they have had to return to providing large-group rather than small-group orientation sessions. She had not considered students as a resource to assist with staffing orientation.

Our framework offers a structure for a set of questions that can guide program and instructional development.

1. What are the sources of tension (in their personal, cultural, economic, and social past and present circumstances) for specific students? How can the program help students respond to those ten-

sions? How can instruction help students develop insight into their tensions?

2. What is the turning point that brings a student to a program at this time and what is its relationship to instructional goals?
3. What have students learned about themselves as learners? How does that match their current program? How can the match be improved?
4. What are the primary relationships in a student's life? How are they affected by the student's developing engagement in literacy practices? How can the program support the student through these changes?
5. How do instruction and evaluation address students' interests in engaging in new literacy practices outside as well as inside the program?
6. What are the issues specific students face as they cross boundaries to engage in new literacy practices? How can the literacy program support the student in boundary-crossing?
7. To what extent are shame and self-blame conditions for specific students? How can the program assist students in developing a critical perspective that places their problems with literacy in a broader sociocultural analysis?
8. To what extent are students experiencing changes in self-esteem and identity with more extensive engagement in literacy practices? How can the program support students through this process?
9. How does the program support intensive interaction with a *community* of literate persons? How does the program support student interaction on a regular basis?

We anticipate that many more questions will arise as students and practitioners work together to explore the dimensions of change.

Conclusion

Lawrence, Marsha, Don, Ann, and Maria experience change in their literacy practices to different degrees. Taken together, they help us develop new insights into the process of change and literacy. We propose a framework for change, adapted from Lofland and Stark (1965), with a set of accumulating conditions that describe the process of extensive change adults in our study experienced. Adults:

1. experience enduring, acutely felt tensions in relation to literacy
2. during a time—a turning point—when change feels possible or necessary,
3. which leads them to an educational problem-solving perspective
4. and engagement in an effective instructional program in which affective bonds are formed and relationships outside the program are supportive or neutralized
5. and where the adults are exposed to intensive ongoing interaction in the diverse social and cultural contexts that exist both inside and outside the program.

This framework relies heavily on personal agency; it places the adult learner at the center of the process, and follows the choices that learners make as they engage in literacy education. Tough (1982), examining adults' intentional changes, explains:

> The central importance of the person in his or her own change process became very clear. People usually serve as the manager or navigator of their own intentional changes. They may receive advice, encouragement, and information from other people and books, but they fit this help into their own ongoing self-managed process. . . . The person is an active agent in managing and guiding the process of major change. (p. 55)

We want to recognize that for those adults who manage to experience deep and profound change in their identity as literate people, their own personal resources, perspective, and hard work play a central role. Therefore, our framework is empowering of the individual. Each condition implies resources that the learner brings to the change process, and the accumulation of conditions implies that the learner is active in the social world.

Adults draw on many resources to support pushing and crossing boundaries; these resources can act as conservative conditions that inhibit change as well as forces that propel change. Confidence and social support appear to be primary resources that learners call on in crossing boundaries. Shame appears to be the primary inhibitor of movement.

Many of the adults in our profiles resisted schools' attempts to teach them that they were inadequate (Beder, 1991; Freire & Macedo, 1987; Giroux, 1988; Quigley, 1993); while some sat docilely in the back of the room, drawing pictures and waiting for their time to be served, others acted out, refusing to take the roles the school was handing them. The determination and courage we see in their participation in adult literacy education were forged in the halls of public schools and on the streets of their neighborhoods. These experiences and attitudes can inhibit further learning, or they can act as useful resources for adults who are struggling to hang on to their belief in themselves as they tackle literacy one more time.

At the same time, this framework recognizes the role of other conditions. The tensions, for example, often arise as a result of interaction with a schooling system that was not responsive to these adult's unique situations in childhood. In addition, the larger society's stigma about literacy problems, fueled by the mass media, helps develop a deep sense of shame and difference among many adults who start out on the long road to proficiency in new literacy practices in adulthood.

Many of the adults who experience the first condition of prolonged tension never make it to the second and third sets of conditions because they have been taught that they are unable to learn, or that it is not possible for the world to be different tomorrow from the way it is today. Their deep sense of disillusionment and alienation does not allow for an educational problem-solving perspective or for seeking a solution. In a society beset by racial, class, and gender discrimination, many adults are struggling for survival. The notion of profound change seems just too far away and too dangerous. The literacy program shares responsibility with the learners' communities inside and outside the program for helping adults change.

This framework also divides the social world of adults who are in literacy education into the space inside and outside of literacy programs. Within each of these spaces, situations fall on a continuum ranging from feeling more public to more private; the placement of situations on this sliding scale will change as learners and situations change. In addition, literacy practices within each situation have norms attached to them that provide varying amounts of flexibility in the performance of practices. Those that have the highest stress associated with them usually are practices that follow rigid norms and are conducted in situations that feel quite public and are outside the program. Adults' judgments about their ability to participate in literacy practices may change as the situation or their understanding of the situation changes, as their abilities change, and as their relationship to their own internalized understanding of literacy changes.

In this framework, literacy is not a characteristic of an individual, but has to do with the interaction between an individual and a social setting (Scribner, 1987). Lytle (1991) observes: "A person's literacy profile might be conceptualized as a contemporary quilt in progress, a kind of patchwork whose configuration is closely linked to specific settings characterized by specific opportunities and constraints" (p. 8). As the situations change, literacy use may also change, so, as Lytle explains,

> any individual's quilt will be both unique and dynamic. Rather than positioning literacy development of individuals in relation to a normative framework, then, this perspective suggests that individuals function within complex, interrelated social and cultural systems. (p. 8)

A kaleidoscope may be a truer image, with its patterns shifting continually as the situation and point of view change.

Every time a literacy student tries a new practice, a boundary is pushed. Sometimes a boundary is crossed, such as the first time a literacy student tries a new practice outside the program. Usually, however, the boundaries are pushed; situations that used to feel public begin to feel more private, or the stress of norms is lessened as confidence increases.

Although many adults start out in literacy programs, relatively few actually reach a point of deep, pervasive change in their literacy practices. We understand that many adults bring inner resources to the process that are crucial to success, such as prior experience as learners and a strong vision of the way they want to interact with the social world. On the other hand, many adults' shame and self-blame undermines their ability to learn, and inadequate programs and lack of social and institutional support make movement even more difficult.

We offer an adaptation of Lofland and Stark's (1965) set of conditions as a way of helping us to understand why some adults are able to move through barriers. It poses the adult's inner resources as central to change, but also recognizes that strong relationships inside and outside the program, as well as effective instruction, help learners transform their shame and self-blame and develop positive identities connected to new literacy practices.

Clearly programs can address issues of instruction, curriculum, and culture directly. Staff development can help teachers and tutors develop a perspective on their roles and on the process of change rather than focusing narrowly on techniques. The staff-development process can focus on instructors as learners and as agents of their own learning, providing a model for how teachers would work with their own students (Drennon, 1994; Fingeret & Cockley, 1992; Lytle & Cochran-Smith, 1990, 1992). Instruction can incorporate attention to tasks and practices, and programs can assist students in moving between inside and outside the program and in crossing boundaries. Literacy programs also can help program staff and students learn how to examine culture and become better able to understand the role of culture in their work together. McLaren (1990) reminds us that "a renewed understanding of culture can assist teachers to situate their own classroom practices within larger structure of power and privilege so that they are better able to acknowledge the interests served by their own ideological predilections" (p. 23).

Even with all of these changes, however, many adults will not be able to manage the competing demands of family, job, and school so that they get the kind of immersion that is required for the far-reaching changes they envision in their lives. Policy should support adults' involvement in programs that offer more class time, more "apprentice" time outside the classroom, and more interaction among adults who engage in a wide range of literacy practices. Policy also can support media development of more positive views of adults who want to develop their literacy practices.

In addition, policy can encourage an emphasis on literacy's purposes rather than on discreet goals, engaging practitioners and policymakers in developing a shared vision for literacy. For example, Stein (1995) offers a reshaping of the National Education Goal 6 (National Education Goals Panel, 1994), relating to adult literacy. She calls for policy that will support literacy development for every adult American, emphasizing that an adult must "possess the knowledge and skills necessary to orient oneself in a rapidly changing world, to find one's voice and be heard, and to act independently as a citizen and as a worker, for the good of one's family, one's community and one's nation" (p. 25). The framework we offer can assist in the work toward this goal, helping adult learners and practitioners embrace change throughout their lifetimes.

APPENDIX

Methodology

This book results from a secondary analysis of some of the data originally collected to evaluate Literacy Volunteers of New York City (LVNYC) (Fingeret & Danin, 1991). The purpose of the original study was to develop insight into the impact, for students, of their participation in Literacy Volunteers of New York City in 1990. This was examined in terms of (1) changes in literacy skills; (2) changes in involvement in literacy practices in students' lives; and (3) changes in self-concept related to literacy development. Since the main emphasis was program impact on students, we chose to look at the volunteers and the larger organization primarily in terms of the students' experiences. The original study focused on the program; this book and the secondary analysis focus more directly on the students themselves. In the course of the original study we became particularly intrigued by learners' differing stories of change; this secondary analysis develops additional insights into individual learners' processes of change and presents a framework for change that we hope will be useful to the literacy education field.

Original Evaluation Methodology

Methods to evaluate any program are determined by the stated goals of the program, the purpose of the evaluation, the evaluation questions, and the audience(s) for the evaluation. In 1990, at the time of the original data collection, LVNYC identified itself as committed to student-centered learning that would enhance students' literacy skills as well as have an impact on their self-esteem. Overall, the program hoped to help students create a higher quality of life for themselves and their families. It attempted to reach those goals primarily through literacy instruction, student services, and the Student Leadership Program.

In keeping with the need to access multiple perspectives at multiple sites and to gather data that would help us connect students' experiences with program impacts, the study was primarily qualitative. Qualitative methods provide a holistic view and reveal the program in as naturalistic a way as possible. This is not to say that the evaluation is "value-free" (Lincoln & Guba, 1985), but that analysis is inductive rather than deductive. Qualitative research is descriptive and is concerned with process as well as outcome (Bogdan & Biklen, 1982; Patton, 1980).

All evaluation research must meet certain criteria for rigorous and systematic investigation in order to be useful. Qualitative inquiry must meet the criteria of credibility, transferability, dependability, and confirmability (Lincoln & Guba, 1985). Credibility of findings and interpretations can most likely be ensured by prolonged engagement on-site, persistent observation, triangulation, peer debriefing, negative case analysis, and member checking. The remaining criteria depend, to a large extent, on establishing credibility. The evaluation, by design, met these criteria.

The evaluation project was completed in three phases: (1) planning, (2) data collection, and (3) data analysis and validation. During the planning phase, the Principal Investigator met with the staff, Executive Director, program committee of the board, and Student Advocates (former students on staff in the central office who form the Student Leadership Team) to identify the evaluation questions and goals. The Advisory Committee was established to work with the evaluators to provide input on the evaluation process and to serve as a check on credibility. The Advisory Committee consisted of three staff members, two students, one tutor, and two board members.

The field research team consisted of the Principal Investigator, the Project Director, and three on-site fieldworkers. The Principal Investigator and/or Project Director met with the evaluation Advisory Committee during each of the three phases and consulted with individual committee members as needed during the project. They also met with the Executive Director and/or with the Director of Education about once a month during data collection and preliminary analysis to ensure open communication. These various meetings are examples of peer debriefing and member checking, which are necessary to establish credibility.

Data Collection

We used open-ended focus group interviews, individual interviews, and observation as the main data collection methods. Additional data included students' demographic information, standardized test scores, and writing samples. All program documents were made available to us, including the tutor training manual, student advocate guidelines, past internal and external evaluations, data forms, and minutes of the Student Committee meetings. We also collected samples of the various newsletters produced by each of the centers and LVNYC publications.

Focus group interviews were conducted with one instructional group from each of the nine instructional programs, located in seven centers. Focus group interviews are conducted because they allow the participants to interact with and respond to each other around a specified topic, experience in the literacy program in this case, and provide greater understanding of why certain views are held (Krueger, 1988). All participants were assured of confidentiality.

The Principal Investigator and the Project Director conducted a pilot focus group interview to test the questions and made some additions based on students' responses. Two of the fieldworkers who had previous field research experience in educational settings accompanied either the Principal Investigator or the Project Director on an interview and observation, to assure reliability in data collection. These fieldworkers were responsible for seven student focus group interviews and follow-up observations, the case studies interviews, and one tutor training observation. The third fieldworker conducted telephone interviews of students identified by the program as dropouts and conducted the interview of the Student Committee together with the Project Director. The Project Director and/or Principal Investigator conducted the remainder of the personal interviews, focus groups, and observations.

The focus group interviews were conducted without the tutor(s) present. At a later date, the fieldworker observed the same group on site during an instructional session and conducted a debriefing interview with the tutor. All interviews were unstructured and focused on the general themes of students' goals, experiences in the program, and changes in literacy skills and practices inside and outside the program. All interviews were audiorecorded and lasted from 1½ to 2 hours.

Two additional student groups were interviewed at the request of the Advisory Committee. These groups differed from the intact instructional groups because they were composed of students from multiple groups at two of the larger centers. The assumption was that the intact groups would provide depth of experience while the heterogeneous groups would provide breadth of experience. There also was a concern that members of intact groups might already have negotiated their norms; topics that might be aired elsewhere could be taboo in such settings. On the other hand, it was possible that intact groups would support their members in talking about painful or difficult topics that would otherwise not surface. Interestingly, the responses from the two types of groups were very similar and provided important evidence for credibility and dependability.

Individual student volunteers were selected from the nine intact groups to participate in case studies. The case studies afforded greater opportunity to explore the students' experience in a broader context and in greater depth. Nine of the students were interviewed outside of their center and, in four of the cases, the fieldworker interviewed either a family member(s) or friend as well. A 10th case study was added because one student left the program before all the interviews were completed. Case studies involved either two or three additional interviews of 1½ to 2 hours each. They also often included opportunities for the students to share their writing notebooks or folders with the fieldworker and to discuss their writing at length.

Focus group interviews also were conducted with the Student Committee, one transition group, one group of graduates from the program, the Tutor Committee, and center directors. All of the Interview Guides and more detailed descriptions of sample demographics can be found in the original report (Fingeret & Danin, 1991).

We also collected data that would help us understand how tutors are being prepared and how students are being oriented to the program. We observed tutor training sessions and we attended a program-wide event, an annual celebration of students' writing.

Finally, interviews were conducted with key staff members: three student advocates who are former LVNYC students, the coordinator for tutor training, the coordinator of the Preenrollment Program, the coordinator of center directors, the coordinator for the transition group, the Evaluation Director, the Education Director, and the Executive Director. Thus, we were able to triangulate data through multiple sources of information and multiple methods of data collection.

Group interviews and observations began in February and continued through July 1990. Students, volunteers, and staff participated with enthusiasm throughout the data collection process. We were welcomed at all sites and students reported that they enjoyed talking with us. It is common to anticipate an initial awkwardness, but we found that people were open and forthcoming. We tried to invite participation and to convey the inherent flexibility of this kind of responsive research and our concern that they feel that their perspectives were understood and that their issues were being incorporated.

We also collected information that would be analyzed quantitatively, to complement the qualitative body of the study. These data included students' writing samples, taken at different points in their participation in the program, and students' standardized test scores. We agreed to collect data that already were being generated in the program, since students were required to take standardized tests at 50-hour intervals and were writing on a regular basis (see Fingeret & Danin, 1991, for a more extensive discussion of the quantitative data collection and analysis procedures).

Data Analysis and Validation

Qualitative and quantitative data were analyzed separately; the findings in each domain were used to inform the other, to assist with interpretation, and to contribute to the overall conclusions. We were not able to analyze for specific issues relating to gender, race, culture, native language, or age within the scope of this study.

"Analysis is the process of bringing order to data, organizing what is there into patterns, categories, and basic descriptive units" (Patton, 1980, p. 268). Analysis in the qualitative aspects of the evaluation began with the conceptualization of the questions during the planning phase and continued throughout. The formulation of the research questions revealed program staff's, board members', and evaluators' frameworks for what was meaningful and valued. Patton (1980) refers to this process as making theoretical predispositions explicit.

Data collection and analysis are iterative and recursive processes that occurred throughout the evaluation. As the fieldworkers completed interviews and observations and corrected transcripts, they were asked to write up their impressions, and the entire evaluation team discussed what we were finding during our monthly meetings. Our meetings with the Advisory Committee provided further opportunities to discuss themes that we saw during interviews and observations. This ongoing analysis informed the continuing data collection. For example, observations at the program sites revealed a greater variety of activity than "just" reading and writing; we saw groups engaged in math tutoring, training for driver's education, and Bible study. This led to discussion with program staff and collection of additional documents and interview data.

As themes emerged from the experience of one group of participants, we sought to better understand them through interaction with other participants or through documents. For example, we explored themes from the group interviews in more depth during our case study interviews. We were able to compare, contrast, and triangulate data because we interviewed persons across all of the centers and included different levels of perspectives (multiple sources), reviewed documents, and conducted observations (multiple methods) (Patton, 1980).

Coding is a systematic process for "bringing order" to data by identifying and naming patterns and recurring themes. The coding process involved the Principal Investigator and the Project Director, each of whom began with three different focus group interviews and observations. We did an inductive analysis, which meant that the categories or codes came from the data. Our categories reflected the participants' views, feelings, and words. We read through the files and made notes about what and how students talked about their participation in LVNYC. For example, students talked about how they came to the program, what their goals were, and changes they had seen in themselves. These topics became codes, which were subsequently applied to other data and additions or changes were made where necessary until the best match was found between the data and the categories. The Principal Investigator and the Project Director then met to compare coding systems and made further modifications. We returned to the original evaluation questions to make sure we were focusing on relevant data. Once we reached consensus in coding, we conducted a preliminary analysis of the data. The Principal Investigator reviewed a sample of data across the entire program and the Project Director did a more in-depth analysis on a smaller sample. We met again to discuss findings and organize our preliminary analysis according to the evaluation questions.

The preliminary analysis was presented to three groups of people at LVNYC for their response and verification. At this stage we had not completed the writing-task or test-score analyses. We were interested in knowing if what we were finding "made sense" to the study participants: Could they recognize their own experience? In September, we met with the Executive Director, the Education Director, and a Student Advocate for almost 4 hours, with the evaluation Advisory Committee for almost 3 hours, and with the on-site fieldworkers for more than 2 hours. All of these meetings continued past their scheduled closure times as students, staff, fieldworkers, board members, and the evaluation research team worked together to better understand the meaning of what we had seen and heard. We welcomed questions, comments, challenges, and disagreements. All sessions were audiorecorded. The practice of asking participants or stakeholders to review data, interpretations, and conclusions to see if they ring true to them is known as member checking (Lincoln & Guba, 1985); it is a widely used means for validation and verification, which are important for assuring the trustworthiness of the analysis. Each group thought the data were presented clearly, accurately, and fairly, and were congruent with their experiences; the conversations helped us deepen our analysis and directed our attention to specific areas.

On confirmation that analysis was proceeding along the right track, we continued to read transcripts and field notes and code the remaining data. We began with student data from group interviews, observation, and individual case studies. Then we worked with tutor data from interviews and observations during instructional sessions, tutor committee, and tutor training. Finally we turned to the staff interviews and observations. We set up two interpretation sessions and began to outline the final report and make writing assignments. We developed a broad conceptual scheme for impact; we also explored the literature on leadership development, the role of context in development, and organizational theory. The data were reexamined for theoretical validation. We generated recommendations based on our analyses and interpretations.

The Executive Director and the Education Director responded to the first draft of this final report, checking for accuracy. In addition, we were concerned about our promises of confidentiality to some students whose characteristics might be recognizable in the report. We contacted those students and shared with them how their comments were included in the report. We worked with them to make sure they felt comfortable with the report; they also provided additional validation for our analysis. The final report was submitted in 1991 to the Board of Directors of Literacy Volunteers of New York City, and accepted.

Toward a Framework for Change

The depictions of the domains of inside and outside the program from the original evaluation study were particularly useful; they were presented at numerous professional conferences and meetings with literacy students and practitioners. The conception of the role of shame that was developed in the original evaluation was useful for informing staff development as well as instructional efforts. As the original principal investigator, Hanna Fingeret, worked with the concepts (with the staff of Literacy South in Durham, NC) that emerged from the original evaluation, she became increasingly interested in the students' processes of change and the roles of personal, instructional, and environmental conditions. She and Susan Danin, the original Project Director, decided to refocus new writing around the students' experiences rather than around the program. This was originally intended to be an editing process.

Cassie Drennon joined the team as the manuscript began to develop. At the same time, Hanna and Susan began to realize that the original analysis was inadequate for the new focus of the writing. Therefore, Cassie and Hanna conducted a new, inductive analysis of selected parts of the original data. Specifically, the case study interviews were reanalyzed since the new focus was on the students who were included as case studies in the original evaluation (and some of whom are included as profiles in this book). All of the original data, analysis, and writing were used in this new project, as well as the new analysis of the case study interviews. No new data were collected; we attempted to conduct additional interviews with one of the original case study participants, but we were unable to locate him. Analysis was inductive, as in the original study.

Preliminary conceptions of the framework were presented to groups of graduate students and faculty at the University of Georgia in Athens, Georgia, and their response helped refine the emerging framework. In addition, Cassie presented preliminary conceptions of the framework to three groups of literacy students and practitioners in Georgia and Virginia and we incorporated their feedback. Cassie also conducted three workshops with literacy students and practitioners that incorporated aspects of focus groups; these were opportunities to explore the implications of the framework we were developing. Parts of these sessions were audiotaped and the tapes were analyzed; the data are included in the section on implications.

References

Aslanian, C. B., & Brickell, H. M. (1980). *Americans in transition: Life changes as reasons for adult learning.* Princeton: College Board.

Atkins, J., Day, T., Shore, L., & Simon, P. (1990). *A report on using an integrated support services and counseling model in a community college adult basic education project.* Oakland, CA: Center for Working Life.

Auerbach, E. R. (1992). *Making meaning, making change: Participatory curriculum development for adult ESL literacy.* Washington, DC: Center for Applied Linguistics.

Beder, H. (1991). *Adult literacy: Issues for policy and practice.* Malabar, FL: Krieger Publishing Co.

Bogdan, R. C., & Biklen, S. K. (1982). *Qualitative research for education.* Boston: Allyn and Bacon.

Bradshaw, J. (1988). *Healing the shame that binds you.* Deerfield Beach, FL: Health Communications Inc.

Brown, J. S., Collins, A., & Duguid, P. (1989, January-February). Situated cognition and the culture of learning. *Educational Researcher, 18,* 32–42.

Candy, P. C. (1991). *Self-direction for lifelong learning.* San Francisco: Jossey-Bass.

Center for Literacy Studies. (1992). *Life at the margins: Profiles of adults with low literacy skills. Report to the US Congress for the Office of Technology Assessment.* Knoxville, TN: Center for Literacy Studies, University of Tennessee at Knoxville.

D'Amico-Samuels, D. (1991). *Perspectives on assessment from the New York City Adult Literacy Initiative: A critical issues paper.* New York: Literacy Assistance Center.

Darkenwald, G. G., & Valentine, T. (1984). *Outcomes and impact of adult basic education.* New Brunswick, NJ: Center for Adult Development, Rutgers University. (ERIC Document Reproduction Service No. ED 244 135)

Drennon, C. E. (1994). *Inquiry and action: A plan for adult education staff and professional development in Virginia* (rev. ed.). Richmond, VA: State Dept. of Education. (ERIC Document Reproduction Service No: ED371236)

Ehringhaus, C. (1991). Teachers' perceptions of testing in adult basic education. *Adult Basic Education, 3,* 38–155.

Ellsworth, E. (1989, August). Why doesn't this feel empowering? Working through the repressive myths of critical pedagogy. *Harvard Educational Review, 59,* 297–324.

Farr, R., & Carey, R. F. (1986). *Reading: What can be measured* (2nd ed.). Newark, DE: International Reading Association.

Ferdman, B. M. (1990). Literacy and cultural identity. *Harvard Educational Review, 60,* 181–204.

Fingeret, A. (1982). *The illiterate underclass: Demythologizing an American stigma.* Unpublished doctoral dissertation, Syracuse University, Syracuse, NY.

Fingeret, A. (1983, Spring). Social network: A new perspective on independence and illiterate adults. *Adult Education Quarterly, 33,* 133–146.

Fingeret, A. (1992). *Adult literacy education: Current and future directions: An update.* Columbus, OH: ERIC Clearinghouse on Adult, Career, and Vocational Education.

Fingeret, H. (1993). *It belongs to me: A guide to portfolio assessment in adult education programs.* Durham, NC: Literacy South, Inc.

Fingeret, H., & Cockley, S. (1992). *Teachers learning: Evaluation of ABE teacher training in Virginia.* Richmond, VA: Adult Literacy Resource Center.

Fingeret, H., & Danin, S. (1991). *They really put a hurtin' on my brain: Learning in Literacy Volunteers of New York City.* New York: Literacy Volunteers of NYC.

Fingeret, H., Tom, A., Dyer, P., Morley, A., Dawson, J., Harper, L., Lee, D., McCue, M., & Niks, M. (1994). *Lives of change: An ethnographic evaluation of two learner centered literacy programs.* Ottawa, Canada: National Literacy Secretariat.

Firestone, R. W. (1988). *Voice therapy.* New York: Human Sciences Press.

Foster, L. (1989). *Self esteem and mental imagery in the ABE classroom: A holistic perspective.* Unpublished masters qualifying paper, North Carolina State University, Raleigh.

Freire, P. (1985). *The politics of education.* South Hadley, MA: Bergin and Garvey.

Freire, P., & Macedo, D. (1987). *Literacy: Reading the word and the world.* South Hadley, MA: Bergin and Garvey.

Giroux, H. A. (1988). *Schooling and the struggle for public life: Critical pedagogy in a modern age.* Minneapolis: University of Minnesota Press.

Goldberg, C. (1991). *Understanding shame.* Northvale, NJ: Jason Aronson Inc.

Heath, S. B. (1980, Winter). The functions and uses of literacy. *Journal of Communication, 30,* 123–133.

Heath, S. B. (1983). *Ways with words: Language, life and work in communities and classrooms.* New York: Cambridge University Press.

Horsman, J. (1991). *Something in my mind besides the everyday: Women and literacy.* Toronto, Canada: Women's Press.

Hunter, L. (1990). *A search for the meaning of becoming literate: An interpretive inquiry.* Ottawa, Canada: National Literacy Secretariat.

Kaufman, G. (1985). *Shame: The power of caring.* Cambridge, MA: Schenkman Books.

Klassen, C. (1991). Bilingual written language use by low-education Latin American newcomers. In D. Barton & R. Ivanic (Eds.), *Writing in the community* (pp. 38–57). Newbury Park, CA: Sage Publications.

Krueger, R. A. (1988). *Focus groups: A practical guide for applied research.* Beverly Hills, CA: Sage Publications.

Lincoln, Y. S., & Guba, E. G. (1985). *Naturalistic inquiry.* Beverly Hills, CA: Sage Publications.

Lofland, J., & Lofland, L. (1995). *Analyzing social settings: A guide to qualitative observation and analysis* (3rd ed.). Belmont, CA: Wadsworth Publishing.

Lofland, J., & Stark, R. (1965). Becoming a world-saver: A theory of conversion to a deviant perspective. *American Sociological Review, 30*, 862–874.

Lytle, S. L. (1991). Living literacy: Rethinking development in adulthood. *Linguistics and Education, 3*, 109–138.

Lytle, S. L., & Cochran-Smith, M. (1990, Fall). Learning from teacher research: A working typology. *Teachers College Record, 92*, 83–103.

Lytle, S. L., & Cochran-Smith, M. (1992). Teacher research as a way of knowing. *Harvard Educational Review, 62*, 447–474.

Lytle, S. L., & Wolfe, M. (1989). *Adult literacy education: Program evaluation and learner assessment.* Columbus, OH: ERIC Clearinghouse on Adult, Career, and Vocational Education, Ohio State University.

McLaren, P. (1990). Radical pedagogy: Constructing an arch of social dreaming and a doorway to hope. In G. J. Conti & R.A. Fellenz (Eds.), *Social environment and adult learning* (pp. 19–35). Bozeman, MT: Kellogg Center for Adult Learning Research, Montana State University.

Merriam, S. B., & Caffarella, R. S. (1991). *Learning in adulthood.* San Francisco: Jossey-Bass.

Mezirow, J. (1991). *Transformative dimensions in adult learning.* San Francisco: Jossey-Bass.

Mezirow, J. (1996). Contemporary paradigms of learning. *Adult Education Quarterly, 46*, 158–173.

Nash, A., Cason, A., Rhum, M., McGrail, L., & Gomez-Sanford, R. (1992). *Talking shop: A curriculum sourcebook for participatory adult ESL.* Washington, DC: Center for Applied Linguistics.

National Education Goals Panel. (1994). *National education goals report.* Washington, DC: Government Printing Office.

Parker, J. M. (1991). *A story of two urban black women learning to read.* Unpublished doctoral dissertation, New York University, New York, NY.

Patton, M. Q. (1980). *Qualitative evaluation methods.* Beverly Hills, CA: Sage Publications.

Paulson, F. L., Paulson, P. R., & Meyer, C. A. (1991). What makes a portfolio a portfolio? *Educational Leadership, 48*, 60–63.

Pratt, D. D. (1990). Contrasting foundations for learning and teaching: Selfhood in China and the United States. In G. J. Conti & R.A. Fellenz (Eds.), *Cultural influences on adult learning* (pp. 29–44). Bozeman, MT: Kellogg Center for Adult Learning Research, Montana State University.

Quigley, A. (1993, Summer). Seeking a voice: Resistance to schooling and literacy. *Adult Basic Education, 3*, 77–90.

Reder, S. M. (1987). Comparative aspects of functional literacy development: Three ethnic communities. In D. Wagner (Ed.), *The future of literacy in a changing world* (Vol. 1, pp. 250–270). Oxford: Pergamon.

Reder, S. M., & Green, K. R. (1985). *Giving literacy away.* Portland, OR: Northwest Regional Laboratory. (ERIC Document Reproduction Service No. ED 253 775)

Resnick, L. B. (1987, December). Learning in school and out. *Educational Researcher*, *45*, 13–19.

Sanford, L. T., & Donovan, M. E. (1984). *Women and self-esteem*. New York: Penguin.

Scribner, S. (1987). Introduction to theoretical perspectives on comparative literacy. In D. Wagner (Ed.), *The future of literacy in a changing world* (Vol. 1, pp. 19–24). Oxford: Pergamon Press.

Scribner, S., & Cole, M. (1981). *The psychology of literacy*. Cambridge, MA: Harvard University Press.

Shor, I. (Ed.). (1987). *Freire for the classroom: A sourcebook of liberatory teaching*. Portsmouth, NH: Boynton/Cook Publishers.

Soifer, R., Irwin, M. E., Crumrine, B. M., Honzaki, E., Simmons, B. K., & Young, D. L. (1990). *The complete theory-to-practice handbook of adult literacy: Curriculum design and teaching approaches*. New York: Teachers College Press.

Stein, S. G. (1995). *Equipped for the future: A customer-driven vision for adult literacy and lifelong learning*. Washington, DC: National Institute for Literacy.

Stein, S. G. (1997). *Equipped for the future: A reform agenda for adult literacy and lifelong learning*. Washington, DC: National Institute for Literacy.

Sticht, T. G. (1990). *Testing and assessment in adult basic education and English as a second language programs*. San Diego, CA: Applied Behavioral & Cognitive Sciences, Inc.

Strauss, R. (1976). Changing oneself: Seekers and the creative transformation of life experience. In J. Lofland (Ed.), *Doing social life* (pp. 252–272). New York: John Wiley.

Street, B. (1992). *Literacy in theory and practice*. New York: Cambridge University Press.

Tierney, R. J., Carter, M. A., & Desai, L. E. (1991). *Portfolio assessment in the reading-writing classroom*. Norwood, MA: Christopher Gordon Publishers.

Tough, A. (1982). *Intentional changes*. Chicago: Follett.

Valencia, S. (1990). A portfolio approach to classroom reading assessment: The whys, whats, and hows. *The Reading Teacher*, *43*, 338–340.

Weinstein-Shr, G. (1990). From problem-solving to celebration: Discovering and creating meaning through literacy. *TESL Talk*, *20*, 68–88.

Wolf, D. P. (1989). Portfolio assessment: Sampling student work. *Educational Leadership*, *46*, 35–39.

Wrigley, H. S., & Guth, G. J. A. (1992). *Bringing literacy to life: Issues and options in adult ESL literacy*. San Mateo, CA: Aguirre International.

Ziegahn, L. (1990). The formation of literacy perspective. In G. J. Conti & R. A. Fellenz (Eds.), *Adult learning in the community* (pp. 1–31). Bozeman, MT: Kellogg Center for Adult Learning Research, Montana State University.

Index

About the Authors

Hanna Arlene Fingeret, Ph.D., has worked as a literacy practitioner and has served on the faculty of North Carolina State University. She is the former executive director of Literacy South in Durham, NC, and has written extensively about adult literacy education.

Cassandra Drennon is the former Senior Staff Development Specialist for adult literacy in Virginia. She currently is a doctoral student in adult education at the University of Georgia, Athens, Georgia, and consultant to Literacy South, Durham, NC.